P9-BJO-733

Arthur M. Cohen
EDITOR-IN-CHIEF

Florence B. Brawer
ASSOCIATE EDITOR

Accreditation of the Two-Year College

Carolyn Prager
Franklin University

EDITOR

WITHDRAWN

Number 83, Fall 1993

JOSSEY-BASS PUBLISHERS
San Francisco

Published in cooperation with
ERIC Clearinghouse
for Junior Colleges

EDUCATIONAL RESOURCES INFORMATION CENTER

ERIC Clearinghouse For Junior Colleges

UNIVERSITY OF CALIFORNIA, LOS ANGELES

ACCREDITATION OF THE TWO-YEAR COLLEGE
Carolyn Prager (ed.)
New Directions for Community Colleges, no. 83
Volume XXI, number 3
Arthur M. Cohen, Editor-in-Chief
Florence B. Brawer, Associate Editor

Microfilm copies of issues and articles are available in 16mm and 35mm, as well as microfiche in 105mm, through University Microfilms Inc., 300 North Zeeb Road, Ann Arbor, Michigan 48106.

LC 85-644753   ISSN 0194-3081   ISBN 1-55542-718-9

NEW DIRECTIONS FOR COMMUNITY COLLEGES is part of The Jossey-Bass Higher and Adult Education Series and is published quarterly by Jossey-Bass Inc., Publishers, 350 Sansome Street, San Francisco, California 94104-1310 (publication number USPS 121-710) in association with the ERIC Clearinghouse for Community Colleges. Second-class postage paid at San Francisco, California, and at additional mailing offices. POST-MASTER: Send address changes to New Directions for Community Colleges, Jossey-Bass Inc., Publishers, 350 Sansome Street, San Francisco, California 94104-1310.

SUBSCRIPTIONS for 1993 cost $49.00 for individuals and $72.00 for institutions, agencies, and libraries.

THE MATERIAL in this publication is based on work sponsored wholly or in part by the Office of Educational Research and Improvement, U.S. Department of Education, under contract number RI-88-062002. Its contents do not necessarily reflect the views of the Department, or any other agency of the U.S. Government.

EDITORIAL CORRESPONDENCE should be sent to the Editor-in-Chief, Arthur M. Cohen, at the ERIC Clearinghouse for Community Colleges, University of California, Los Angeles, California 90024.

Cover photograph © Rene Sheret, After Image, Los Angeles, California, 1990.

The paper used in this journal is acid-free and meets the strictest guidelines in the United States for recycled paper (50 percent recycled waste, including 10 percent post-consumer waste). Manufactured in the United States of America.

039940

Contents

Editor's Notes

Authors have long concluded their prefatory remarks with the date and place of composition, in expectation that readers would attach some significance to the writing's temporal and geographic contexts. In the Information Age, place is more universal and, therefore, of less consequence than it once was, but given the rapidity of change, the date is perhaps more important than ever. These introductory notes were compiled in early April 1993, when the U.S. accreditation structure was reforming in response to internal discord and external discontent (Marchese, 1992; Leatherman, 1992, 1993). As this volume, *Accreditation of the Two-Year College,* went to press, the Council on Postsecondary Accreditation (COPA), the umbrella group for regional, national, and specialized accreditors since 1975, had ceased to exist. And it is still uncertain how the yet unwritten regulations to carry out the Reauthorization of Higher Education Amendments of 1992 will reshape the respective roles that educational institutions, accrediting agencies, and government will take in responding to public demands on colleges and universities for accountability and performance improvement.

In the end, we may come to see our form of accreditation, as Churchill did democracy, as an imperfect system but better than "all those other forms [of government] that have been tried from time to time" (Oxford University Press, 1980, p. 150). The authors represented in this volume appear to assume that the current accreditation associations constitute an imperfect system worth preserving not only because the alternatives are worse, but also because of this form of accreditation's potential to rethink itself and assume a more active and responsive role. How active and how responsive that role becomes, of course, depends to a large extent on what we want it to be.

To help those involved with community colleges examine accreditation's role, several contributors raise accreditation issues of particular importance to two-year colleges. They address pragmatic concerns about consistency, cost, and redundant efforts as well as more strategic issues such as accreditation's potential to provide leadership in such areas as transfer, articulation, and general education. For example, Robert S. Palinchak, Corrinne A. Caldwell, and Lawrence S. Cote ask if it is in the public interest for institutional accreditors to review differently-configured two-year campuses differently, a question that sometimes bears on the campuses' status and recognition as institutions of higher education. In Chapter One, Robert S. Palinchak calls for a more consistent and organic approach to the evaluation of two-year schools by the six regional accrediting associations. He suggests that two-year schools should be evaluated first in terms of characteristics shared with other institutions of higher education, and second in terms of their efficacy as locally based institutions with distinctive delivery modes and student populations. In Chapter Two, Corrinne A. Caldwell and Lawrence S. Cote frame related questions about the accreditation of baccalaureate degree–granting institutions' two-year branch campuses with missions and populations that diverge markedly from those of their parent institutions.

In Chapter Three, I look at accreditation in relation to general education in career curricula. I posit a role for accreditation bodies as change agents, helping institutions to bridge the dual cultures of general and technical studies and of two- and four-year education through more coordinated attention to general learning in both arts and sciences courses and technical courses. The underlying question here and in Chapter Nine is whether accreditation bodies should be more than the sum of their parts.

In Chapter Four, in response to criticisms about accreditation's excessive cost and redundancy, Charles R. Reidlinger and I note that diminishing an institution's participation in accreditation will not necessarily lead to real monetary or qualitative gains. Colleges will still have to hold themselves accountable, or be held accountable by others, through self-study, outcomes analysis and reporting, external review, or other expensive evaluative mechanisms and processes. In this examination of cost-benefit philosophies and methodologies, Reidlinger and I propose ways to reduce the real costs of accreditation while preserving its traditional benefits of self-examination, external scrutiny, and participatory membership.

In recent years, the accreditation community has adopted outcomes assessment to meet the demands for a public accounting of what educators do and how well they do it. In Chapter Five, James C. Palmer examines the fit between assessment designed to examine specific qualitative outcomes and community colleges that are frequently designed to serve diverse populations with as many possible outcomes as there are students. Examining the resulting disjuncture of methods and motives, he foresees the possibility of two-year colleges' changing their structure, organization, and academic expectations in ways that might allow them to accommodate heterogeneous populations less homogeneously than outcomes assessment might seem to require.

In Chapter Six, college president Evan S. Dobelle offers a set of six practical considerations for leading colleges through the accreditation process, starting with the president's need to build consensus before the eleventh hour. In Chapter Seven, college president Eduardo J. Marti offers complementary pragmatic advice for garnering collegiate as well as community goodwill from the accreditation process.

As G. Jeremiah Ryan points out in Chapter Eight, most faculty and many staff are internally focused and do not hear the steady chorus of public demands for change in how educators validate what they do. Along with Dobelle and Marti, Ryan stresses that accreditation's potential to transform the academic decision-making culture and climate depends greatly on presidential abilities to lead by example in building consensus, empowering faculty and staff, sharing governance, and accepting criticism. He calls college leaders' attention, in particular, to the academic culture's sensitivity to language, probity, and utility.

In Chapter Nine, Howard L. Simmons emphasizes the essentially complementary, or symbiotic, relationship of the regional accreditors to the accredited, and the nature of accreditors as entities functioning by the consent of the governed. In his examination of accreditation's limits and potential, he also cautions colleges to think carefully about the alternatives to peer accreditation implicit in recent federal legislation.

Finally, in Chapter Ten, David Deckelbaum presents an annotated bibliography of current resources for the community college accreditation process.

Taken together, these chapters provide varied institutional and global perspectives on accreditation. They acknowledge accreditation's considerable strengths and also cite its weaknesses. Each chapter is intended, in its respective way, to further dialogue about accreditation in general and its impact on the two-year college in particular.

Carolyn Prager
Editor

References

Leatherman, C. "Role of Accreditation Questioned Following a Storm of Criticism and Debate." *Chronicle of Higher Education,* Feb. 19, 1992, pp. A15–A16.

Leatherman, C. "6 Regional Groups Say They'll Drop Out of Council on Postsecondary Accreditation." *Chronicle of Higher Education,* Feb. 10, 1993, pp. A15–A16.

Marchese, T. "Regional Accreditation (II)." *Change,* 1992, *24* (2), 4.

Oxford University Press. *The Oxford Dictionary of Quotations.* Oxford, England: Oxford University Press, 1980.

CAROLYN PRAGER *is dean of the College of Arts and Sciences at Franklin University in Columbus, Ohio.*

Accreditation does what it is traditionally supposed to do, but not what it needs to do today.

Regional Accreditation and Two-Year Colleges

Robert S. Palinchak

No single model or set of standards characterizes two-year college accreditation. Accreditation models and standards vary distinctively among the six geographic accreditation regions that cover the United States and its territories. Without a common set of outcomes to be measured by accreditation, there can be no common understanding or expectations of the accreditation process.

In the United States, the term *postsecondary education* applies to several two-year institutional formats and to shorter training programs in business and industry, in public health and safety agencies, in embalming schools, in the military, and so forth. Increasingly, the trend is for colleges to embrace these noncollegiate programs of study and their nontraditional students as part of higher education. Many colleges routinely evaluate incoming students' postsecondary noncollegiate instruction and award it higher education credit. But the existence of many types of postsecondary providers sometimes challenges the logic of the distinctions made by different regional accreditors about two-year schools that offer similar or related programs.

These distinctions arise because institutional accreditation is carried out by a variety of accrediting commissions that share a guild relationship within each larger regional association. Thus, regional associations are umbrella organizations, meeting member institutions' different needs through different commissions. Similarly configured two-year colleges may be served by a commission for institutions of higher education in one region and by a commission for two-year colleges or vocational-technical institutions in another region. Can a two-year institution receive regional accreditation if it does not offer the associate degree? The answer is yes, no, or perhaps, depending on the institution's geographic region, the historical roots of two-year education and of accrediting practices in the region, the nature of the school, and the kind of diplomas or degrees the school does offer.

Origins of Regional Accreditation

Regional accreditation is deeply rooted in the history of U.S. schooling, and is a largely U.S. invention, conceived of by educators for educators. It arose originally from educators' perceived need to preserve the distinct history, tradition, and quality of four-year colleges and universities. Despite the many changes that have occurred in higher education in this century, accreditation and educational institutions remain interlocked in ways that some call symbiotic and others self-serving (Marchese, 1992).

Different accrediting associations emerged in different geographic regions in response to the pattern in which lower schools and colleges spread throughout the United States, first to New England and the Northeast, then to the Midwestern and Southern areas, and finally to the West. The associations arose primarily to protect the academic virtue, perceived reputation, and institutional integrity of prestigious colleges and universities in the face of a highly differentiated and uncoordinated educational system. Initially, the colleges were most concerned with accrediting the secondary schools that supplied the colleges' students.

The accrediting associations were formed before state governments felt compelled to deal seriously with educating the masses in a relatively classless society. Overall educational direction and leadership was left to the states because there is no mention of education in the U.S. Constitution. The separation of church and state meant that the church could not be a source of uniformity either. Moreover, some states, such as Alabama, had removed education from their state constitutions so as to reduce their perceived obligations to educate minorities. (Accreditation, whatever its considerable merits, has had little discernible influence on producing educational equity, improving access, or reducing educational racism.)

Therefore, the most influential four-year colleges in the regions organized their own membership in accrediting associations for self-preservation and maintenance of the status quo. To assure that a qualified pool of applicants arrived at their doors, they banded together in a protectionist reaction against the local, erratic, and unconditioned growth of public secondary schools and the proliferation of new colleges, many of which were only the equivalent of a decent high school. Regional accreditation rapidly became the means of identifying the "better" high schools: that is, those that adhered to Carnegie unit standards, which required that a subject be studied for a minimum of 120 hours a year. Accreditation thus originally implied that a secondary school was reputable because its graduates could be accepted without reservation by colleges that shared in the overall accreditation process.

The number of public high schools grew rapidly in the 1800s, and these schools' fundamental purpose changed constantly as they debated whether they were preparing students for college or for life. With the rise of vocationalism, particularly in the South and Midwest, comprehensive high schools came to be accepted as the institutions of compromise. As a result, prestigious four-year colleges pressed even harder for a formal, systematic means of identifying and sanctioning those schools that developed appropriate curricula based upon the Carnegie unit. Through the accrediting association relationship, accredited high schools shared a bond with member colleges, and this bond assured the educational community that graduates of accredited high schools could continue their education with a minimum of makeup work or remediation. The fact that only accredited high schools and colleges belonged to the same regional organization implied that the unaccredited were deficient in their academic curricula, possibly because they were too vocational.

Westward Expansion and Vocationalism

The U.S. population's westward expansion encouraged the concept of a basic education for the common citizen who had been overlooked by private and sectarian interests. Just as the Boston Latin Grammar School had taken hold in the Colonial Northeast, little red schoolhouses appeared on the Western prairies. There, time available for schooling had to fit with an agrarian work pattern. The result was an educational calendar that persists today, despite the passing of an agricultural economy—indeed, despite the passing of the subsequent industrial economy. More importantly, the agrarian and industrial economies left a second legacy in the continuing clash between U.S. education's academic and vocational purposes. The various secondary school patterns of development, and their social, political, and economic causes, later encouraged the development of two-year colleges with various missions. For example, some two-year colleges were legislated to address the teacher shortages of the 1960s while others were to serve as a support structure for economic development. And while some were clearly intended to be upward extensions of the comprehensive high school, others were clearly designed to be the freshman and sophomore years of a traditional baccalaureate education. In some states, however, two-year colleges are prohibited from offering transfer programs because to do so would intrude upon the state universities' domain. In other states, universities dominate the delivery of the two-year degree by offering far more programs and support services than the community colleges. In yet other states, technical schools, community colleges, and university branch campuses all offer similar two-year programs and diplomas. In still other states, these three kinds of institutions offer similar two-year programs but different diplomas. And while many community colleges are currently striving to add a substantive vocational dimension to their arts and sciences mission, others are striving to add a meaningful, transferable arts and sciences dimension to a vocational base.

The range of two-year schools currently in existence reflects their diverse origins and missions. The differences between university centers and branch campuses are real. So, too, are the differences between a university community college and one designed as a stand-alone feeder school for grades thirteen and fourteen. While the U.S. regional accreditation system developed from a strong need to separate secondary education from collegiate education and to clarify the standards of secondary education during a period of rapid and undirected growth, the system continues to evolve somewhat indiscriminately in its response to the multiple types of two-year schools.

How do regional accrediting commissions view the many two-year institutions that now flourish? How do they cope with the many substantive differences in mission, outcomes, and funding? How do they deal with proliferation, market saturation, and competition among two-year entities that offer similar services to similar populations? In an era of shrinking resources, the public expense of maintaining redundant educational systems is a salient issue. Yet the public interest in the politics of two-year educational delivery systems is often overlooked. In some locations, one can find a state university two-year branch campus and two community colleges along with a private two-year college, a hospital-based nursing program, and several two-year private for-profit institutions, all operating within a few miles of each other. All might share membership in the same accrediting association, although they may be accredited by different commissions within that association. Some states have elaborate public two-year college systems that do not articulate well with their four-year state colleges and universities. Some even maintain large parallel two-year systems—one for liberal arts and sciences transfer studies and the other for technical education and job training. As Caldwell and Cote discuss at greater length in Chapter Two, a university's two-year center may enjoy accreditation as a result of the blanket accreditation of the parent institution, despite considerable academic and geographic diversity between the center and its parent. However, the region's other two-year community and technical colleges must undergo separate institutional accreditation, which may be performed either by the same accreditation commission that reviews the university or by a separate commission.

Despite the concentration and duplication of two-year providers in some areas, concerns about relative cost, public underwriting, efficiency, effectiveness, and interinstitutional articulation generally fall outside accreditation's scope of action. In such instances, is the public interest well served? Should regional accrediting bodies probe deeper before allowing a two-year school to enjoy accreditation from a commission that does not accredit all comparable schools? Or do the internal composition and operations of accrediting associations so reflect the diversity of structures they evaluate that they cannot respond to these larger public policy questions? As the following information about the six regional accrediting associations shows, their current structures do affect their functioning.

Six Regional Associations

The six regional accreditors are each made up of a variety of quasi-autonomous separate commissions with their own standards, bylaws, and rules of operation. In some regions, this accrediting structure effectively separates arts and sciences degree–granting institutions from vocational ones, or degree-granting institutions from nondegree ones. For example, the programs of many two-year postsecondary vocational-technical institutions are on a par with community college programs except for degree-granting authority. But rather than seek common ground among similar institutions, the accreditation process in such instances yields to the status quo, with little regard to cost effectiveness, unnecessary duplication of services, student interests, or sound public policy.

New England Association of Schools and Colleges. The New England association reviews member institutions at least once every ten years, conducting the business of evaluation and accreditation through five major commissions. Whereas higher education commissions in most other regions generally review all two-year colleges, the New England Association of Schools and Colleges Commission on Institutions of Higher Education (1992) is limited to reviewing schools that award at least one general studies associate degree. The New England Association of Schools and Colleges Commission on Vocational, Technical, and Career Institutions (1982, 1991) has separate standards of membership for specialized institutions of higher education that award an associate degree at the technical or career level, postsecondary institutions that offer only certificates or diplomas, and secondary vocational-technical schools. The higher education commission accredits some thirty-eight two-year colleges, which generally have both degree (Associate in Arts, Associate in Science, and Associate in Applied Science) and nondegree programs. The vocational commission accredits some forty-three two-year colleges plus sixty-five secondary schools with secondary and postsecondary programs. Postsecondary institutions in the New England region can seek accreditation in either one of these two commissions. Comprehensive community colleges, offering both academic and vocational programs, must be accredited by the higher education commission. Obviously, the existence of the two commissions perpetuates the differences various cultural interests have historically made between the liberal arts and sciences and vocational-technical pursuits. Today, when neither educational concept can effectively stand alone, this accreditation structure does little to promote better institutional coexistence.

Independent or private education has long roots in New England. The separate culture that required vocational-technical studies clearly came later and, therefore, had to fit its programs into education's existing socio-economic and political base. Thus, in the New England region, the Associate in Arts and Associate in Science degrees have become the major factor in determining which commission and which culture an institution best fits.

Middle States Association of Colleges and Schools. The Middle States association comprises three commissions, one of which is the Commission on Higher Education (Middle States Association of College and Schools, Commission on Higher Education, 1990). This commission accredits all the institutions of higher education in the Middle States region, unlike the situation in the New England region, where two commissions are at work. The accreditation period is five years for a self-study and five years for a periodic review report. At one time, special criteria for community colleges were used, but no longer. According to the executive director of the Commission on Higher Education, it would be a mistake to treat these institutions differently since it took so long for the other higher education sectors to accept community colleges' legitimacy. In addition, the Middle States association has abandoned its former practice of setting objective, quantifiable standards in favor of making broader statements about integrity, mission, humane policies, admissions policies, resources, qualified faculty, and so forth. As specified in its bylaws, the Commission on Higher Education is expected to accredit, evaluate, and consult in all appropriate ways to promote the welfare and improvement of education with special emphasis on service to member institutions. Also, as in the other regions, the accreditation process rests strictly on an institution's ability to set and meet its own standards, to say what it does and then do what it says. There is no implicit level of performance, no implied comparability of institutions, and no uniformity of process or similarity of aims warranted or expressed.

North Central Association of Colleges and Schools. The North Central association conducts its business through two commissions, one of which is the Commission on Institutions of Higher Education (North Central Association of Colleges and Schools, Commission on Institutions of Higher Education, 1992c), in existence since 1913. The higher education commission does not accredit for a set period; the timing of a comprehensive evaluation is, therefore, always subject to alteration. In practice, however, North Central calls for reaffirmation not later than ten years following each prior reaffirmation, and often uses focused visits and annual reports at shorter intervals.

In the 1920s, North Central's higher education commission differ–entiated its criteria for junior colleges. However, it now accredits all postsecondary institutions and does not differentiate between two- or four-year institutions or between variations of two-year schools, such as community colleges, vocational institutes, technical colleges, two-year university campuses, and other specialized colleges. Recently revised criteria include the requirement that an institution have "clear and publicly stated purposes consistent with its mission and appropriate to an *institution of higher education* [emphasis added]" (North Central Association of Colleges and Schools, Commission on Institutions of Higher Education, 1992a, p. 4). This is a marked change from the previous wording, which referred to a "postsecondary educational institution" (North Central Association of Colleges and Schools, Commission on Institutions of Higher Education, 1992b, p. 1). While this revised requirement bodes well for community colleges, it will remain a dilemma for vocational institutes and technical colleges in light of their historical missions, unless they are willing to internalize the necessary academic changes implied by their inclusion among institutions of higher education.

Southern Association of Colleges and Schools. The Southern association accredits member institutions through four commissions. They include a commission for colleges and, since 1971, one for occupational education. Initial accreditation is for ten years with the requirement that a five-year self-study report be submitted at the midpoint of the accreditation cycle. The self-study seeks to enhance quality of educational programs while the visitation emphasizes institutional effectiveness.

Two-year institutions are accredited by one of these two commissions. The Southern Association of Colleges and Schools Commission on Colleges (1992) has thirteen conditions of institutional eligibility, including a required minimum of fifteen semester hours of general education or liberal arts for associate degree programs (p. 7). The Southern Association of Colleges and Schools Commission on Occupational Education Institutions (1990) was originally formed to accredit a variety of vocational institutions not accredited by other commissions. Among these postsecondary institutions are vocational-technical schools, occupational education institutions, Job Corps centers, and military schools. Secondary vocational institutions can choose to be accredited by the commission on occupational education or the commission for secondary schools. Authority to grant degrees, however, requires a transition to accreditation by the Commission on Colleges.

The lack of accreditation clarity caused by these arrangements is partially rooted in historical differences between vocational and general education. Higher education was bifurcated in the South, along with many other aspects of social life. Thus, vocational or occupational education in the South sometimes appears to parallel other so-called separate but equal practices, but, at the same time, it has worked as an instrument for racial access and personal and local economic development. It is not uncommon to find postsecondary vocational schools that offer typical two-year college courses in business, fire science, computer science, nursing, digital electronics, and so forth without offering college credit or degrees. Such postsecondary schools are a manifestation of a cultural philosophy that says some students should be offered occupational training in the least amount of time with a minimum of general education. These institutions prepare students for job entry rather than a college degree.

Northwest Association of Schools and Colleges. The Northwest association accredits through a commission on colleges and one on schools. Continuing members are not accredited either permanently or for a fixed period. Instead, the standards are that a self-study and external visitation must be conducted at least every ten years and an interim report and visitation every five years. The Northwest Association of Schools and Colleges Commission on Colleges (1992) accredits postsecondary institutions that have characteristics commonly associated with higher education.

Western Association of Schools and Colleges. The Western association was formed in 1962 when several accrediting agencies came together and formed three commissions, two of which are of interest here. The Western Association of Schools and Colleges Accrediting Commission for Community and Junior Colleges (1990) requires member institutions to conduct a self-study, write a report, and undergo peer review every six years. The Western Association of Schools and Colleges Accrediting Commission for Senior Colleges and Universities (1988) prefers a comprehensive review at least every eight years. The Accrediting Commission for Community and Junior Colleges accredits public, private, independent, and proprietary two-year degree-granting schools. This includes for-profit, not-for-profit, religious, and specialized colleges meeting eligibility criteria that include an independent governing board, general education, public disclosure, and so forth.

Accreditation Dilemmas

Educational institutions would benefit from review and revision of regional accreditation processes in three ways: (1) the stature of two-year schools could be more realistically evaluated, (2) the separation between vocational and academic education could begin to be bridged, and (3) transfer of credits could be more systematic.

Stature of Two-Year Schools. Different accreditation bodies accord different statures to two-year schools, depending on regional perceptions of the extent to which the schools are degree granting or non–degree granting, academic or vocational, postsecondary or higher education institutions. In New England, for example, the authority to grant the Associate in Arts degree distinguishes two-year schools that are accredited as institutions of higher education from those that are accredited as secondary and postsecondary vocational institutions. In the Western region, all two-year schools are accredited separately from senior colleges and universities, regardless of any school's offerings.

Vocationalism and Accreditation. Clearly, major divergent ideologies persist and affect the way occupational studies and general education are regarded in some regions. Regional accreditation practices reflect the tensions that divide the vocational from the academic within institutions such as comprehensive community colleges, within sets of institutions such as community colleges and technical schools, and within the accreditation family of regional and specialized educational programs. This dualism may be out of step with the times. The perpetuation of education that is only or mainly vocational may be dysfunctional, serving neither students nor the community well, given today's changing work methods, the emergence of a global economy, a new work ethic, and, indeed, a totally new workforce on the horizon. While public policy is in need of review on this question of the appropriate balance between the vocational and the academic, accreditation associations can do more than reflect the status quo within their regions. They can reshape standards for all two-year education.

Credit Transfer and Articulation. Despite the level of assurance that accreditation implies and despite the prevailing rhetoric that says accreditation safeguards credit transfer, accreditation does little to assure transfer from certain types of regionally accredited institutions to others. This is true especially for students who move from non–degree-granting programs to similar programs that do grant degrees. A student who transfers from a regionally accredited technical program in a noncollegiate institution has no guarantee that the degree-granting program will give credit for the work the student has already completed, even though that work and the learning outcomes are demonstrably similar to coursework and outcomes at the degree-granting institution.

Regional accreditors could support certain national measures, norms, or minimal competencies for basic skills, literacy, professional standards, and so forth that would make regular transfer of credits between accredited institutions more plausible. In the same vein, the six regional associations could coordinate such processes and criteria as sanction procedures, minimal faculty standards, degree standards, credit definitions, and so forth in order to help certify the academic value of credentials earned at one kind of institution for transfer to another.

Regional accreditation's emphasis on intense institutional self-study also makes it easy for both two- and four-year schools to ignore transfer and articulation issues that require interinstitutional coordination and cooperation. There is little in regional association guidelines to encourage two- and four-year institutions to address transfer and articulation activities and efforts during their self-studies. Although some accrediting associations have embraced two-year colleges within the higher education family, they thereby omit scrutiny of the very elements that most closely bind two- and four-year institutions of higher education—transfer and articulation.

Preserver of the Status Quo or Change Agent?

While it can be argued that regional accreditation is voluntary, the fact that accreditation is a condition of access to specific funds (such as federal and state student financial aid) from various government agencies and most charitable trusts and foundations makes institutional accreditation all but mandatory. Thus regional accreditation serves a viable function for two-year colleges. No longer intended to preserve the integrity and reputation of elite colleges and effective high schools, the accreditation process is now generic and applicable to all institutions. Two-year colleges in all forms fit comfortably with their respective accrediting commissions. In two regions where vocational interests have prevailed, accrediting associations have created alternative commissions to accommodate philosophical differences. In short, it can be argued that accreditation does what it has traditionally been expected to do. The problem is that there is disagreement about whether accreditation's traditional roles meet schools' modern needs. Must accreditation simply preserve the status quo, or should it be a change agent?

The strength of two-year colleges does not lie in blind emulation of their four-year counterparts. While sharing critical elements with baccalaureate-granting institutions, two-year colleges are distinguished by their ability to accommodate nontraditional students with a range of academic and work-oriented programs that require effective teaching, different delivery modes, measurable learning, and active rejection of social, cultural, ethnic, and gender stereotypes. In a period of economic restraint, limited public resources, a changing workforce, and a diverse lot of two-year institutions, it may be time for accreditation associations to review two-year colleges in terms of their abilities to articulate unique missions, serve different populations, and deliver innovative programs. It may also be time to define general learning standards for all two-year programs more rigorously and to evaluate two-year schools on the basis of measurable student outcomes, effectiveness with different populations, and ability to meet changing public needs.

References

Marchese, T. "Regional Accreditation (II)." *Change,* 1992, *24* (2), 4.

Middle States Association of Colleges and Schools, Commission on Higher Education. *Characteristics of Excellence: Revised.* Philadelphia: Middle States Association of Colleges and Schools, 1990.

New England Association of Schools and Colleges, Commission on Institutions of Higher Education. *Standards for Accreditation.* Winchester, Mass.: New England Association of Schools and Colleges, 1992.

New England Association of Schools and Colleges, Commission on Vocational, Technical, and Career Institutions. *General Education Requirements in Specialized Programs*. Winchester, Mass.: New England Association of Schools and Colleges, 1982.

New England Association of Schools and Colleges, Commission on Vocational, Technical, and Career Institutions. *Standards for Membership for Specialized Institutions of Higher Education Awarding an Associate Degree at the Technical or Career Level*. Winchester, Mass.: New England Association of Schools and Colleges, 1991.

North Central Association of Colleges and Schools, Commission on Institutions of Higher Education. *Adopted Revisions of the General Institutional Requirements, the Criteria for Accreditation, and the Candidacy Program*. Chicago: North Central Association of Colleges and Schools, 1992a.

North Central Association of Colleges and Schools, Commission on Institutions of Higher Education. *Explanations of the Proposed Criteria for Accreditation*. Chicago: North Central Association of Colleges and Schools, 1992b.

North Central Association of Colleges and Schools, Commission on Institutions of Higher Education. *A Handbook of Accreditation: 1992–93*. Chicago: North Central Association of Colleges and Schools, 1992c.

Northwest Association of Schools and Colleges, Commission on Colleges. *Accreditation Handbook: 1992 Edition*. Seattle, Wash: Northwest Association of Schools and Colleges, 1992.

Southern Association of Colleges and Schools, Commission on Colleges. *Criteria for Accreditation*. Decatur, Ga.: Southern Association of Colleges and Schools, 1992.

Southern Association of Colleges and Schools, Commission on Occupational Education Institutions. *The Policy and Standards of the Commission on Occupational Education Institutions, 1991 Edition*. Decatur, Ga.: Southern Association of Colleges and Schools, 1990.

Western Association of Schools and Colleges, Accrediting Commission for Community and Junior Colleges. *Handbook of Accreditation and Policy Manual*. Aptos, Calif.: Western Association of Schools and Colleges, 1990. 139 pp. (ED 324 056)

Western Association of Schools and Colleges, Accrediting Commission for Senior Colleges and Universities. *Handbook of Accreditation*. Oakland, Calif.: Western Association of Schools and Colleges, 1988.

ROBERT S. PALINCHAK *is campus dean of the Milwaukee Area Technical College West Campus.*

Accreditation of two-year branch campuses should be considered in relation to accreditation of other programs extended from a college's central campus.

Accreditation and Two-Year Branch Campuses

Corrinne A. Caldwell, Lawrence S. Cote

What constitutes a site for higher education? Is the person who takes a videotape-based credit course at home pursuing a college education? Clearly, yes. Is the living room in which the videotape is viewed a site of the institution granting the credit? Probably not. Consider twenty engineers in a makeshift worksite classroom participating in a satellite-delivered graduate engineering program that originates three thousand miles away. Is their classroom a site of the great research university from which the transmission originates? Obviously, definitions of what constitutes a site can form a long and wide continuum. A large part of this continuum is occupied by myriad possible branch campus arrangements, and, more and more, accrediting agencies must sort out the complex identities of institutions with multiple delivery systems and locations. Although the difficulties of multisite accreditation have long troubled practitioners, neither scholars nor practitioners have published much about the problem. Thrash (1979) provides one of the few statements of the issues involved when she defines questions related to evaluation methods and quality indicators. However, the current literature lacks even basic descriptive compilations of the accrediting associations' policies and practices regarding multiple sites and off-site extensions. Given this dearth of published material, we have set as our modest goal in this chapter to describe existing accreditation policies and procedures that affect one particular part of the site continuum, the two-year campuses of predominantly baccalaureate and graduate degree–granting universities. We analyze the efficacy of these policies and procedures from the regional commissions' perspectives, which we gained through review of the commissions' written policies and through lengthy telephone surveys.

NEW DIRECTIONS FOR COMMUNITY COLLEGES, no. 83, Fall 1993   © Jossey-Bass Publishers   17

The exercise of cataloging and describing existing policies and procedures shows a wide variability in regional accrediting commission response to the challenges posed by multisite institutions. Variations exist on almost every point to be considered, ranging from the definition of branch campus and of that campus's relative autonomy to the process by which the entity may or may not be deemed an accreditable unit. These regional differences persist despite the common historical denominator provided in the 1970s by guidelines established by the Federation of Regional Accrediting Commissions of Higher Education (FRACHE), one of the precursors of the Council on Postsecondary Accreditation. Most commissions used the FRACHE guidelines as the original framework for their regional policies. However, this framework permitted and even encouraged much latitude. In addition, since the 1970s, some commissions have undergone so much change that they appear to have lost their knowledge of this joint precursor to regional policies.

Regional Accreditation Policies and Procedures

In our analysis, we evaluated each commission's policies, practices, and responses on three continua: how the commission defined an individually accredited site, how it determined a site's independence from the parent institution for accreditation purposes, and how it reviewed a branch campus.

Middle States Association of Colleges and Schools, Commission on Higher Education. For the Middle States Commission on Higher Education, "an operationally separate unit is considered to be one which, under the general control of the parent institution, has a core of full-time faculty, a separate student body, a resident administration, and offers a program through which a student may complete all the requirements for a degree either awarded through the unit directly [or] by the parent institution, and has a significant voice in the allocation and management of institutional resources which support [the unit]" (Middle States Association of Colleges and Schools, Commission on Higher Education, 1991b, p. 1). Compared to the other commissions' policies, the Middle States commission's statement is relatively clear. However, this definition of an operationally separate unit leaves ample room for institutional and commission negotiation.

The Middle States Commission on Higher Education has also developed guidelines that inform evaluators of special multisite considerations. This regional commission's policy relies heavily on validating the quality of individual institutional units, and the guidelines state that "each unit must be viewed in its relationship to the total system, but its educational effectiveness can best be assessed by devoting attention to its particular endeavors" (Middle States Association of Colleges and Schools, Commission on Higher Education, 1991a, p. 1). The commission also allows for global review of an institution as a single entity: "When an institution has more than one campus or has operationally separate units the commission may accredit it as a whole, may accredit one or more of its units separately, or may accredit some of its units and not others" (Middle States Association of Colleges and Schools, Commission on Higher Education, 1991b, p. 1). According to the commission's publication *Characteristics of Excellence*, this flexibility is valid because "the forms of educational institutions are less important than their functions" (Middle States Association of Colleges and Schools, Commission on Higher Education, 1990, p. 11). There is no written policy for the actual process of determining the autonomy of a campus unit, and this fact suggests that such a determination may result from institutional and association negotiation. Another commission document notes that, when various locations or discrete units exist, a process of "consultation with the institution [will determine] the manner in which evaluation will be carried out and accreditation designated" (Middle States Association of Colleges and Schools, Commission on Higher Education, 1984, p. 3).

New England Association of Schools and Colleges, Commission on Institutions of Higher Education. The New England Commission on Institutions of Higher Education specifically addresses multisite issues under the commission's standard for organization and governance: "In multi-campus systems, the division of responsibility and authority between the system and the institution is clear; system policies are clearly defined and equitably administered" (New England Association of Schools and Colleges, Commission on Institutions of Higher Education, 1992, p. 7). However, the definition of a multicampus system appears not in this document but in a 1972 supplemental publication that seems to derive directly from its FRACHE antecedent. The criteria for operationally separate institutions include operating under the control of a central administration; having a core of full-time faculty, a separate student body, and a resident administration; and offering programs comprising a totality of educational experience as defined by the appropriate accrediting commission. The commission explicitly states that the determination of a separately accreditable unit and the site visit process depends on negotiation. "Where an institution conducts operations in a variety of locations or through a number of discrete units, the Commission will arrange in consultation with the institution the manner in which evaluation will be carried out and accreditation designated" (New England Association of Schools and Colleges, Commission on Institutions of Higher Education, 1972, p. 3).

North Central Association of Colleges and Schools, Commission on Institutions of Higher Education. The North Central commission's accreditation handbook contains a clearly stated policy of accreditation inclusiveness: "The accreditation of an institution includes all of its components, wherever located. A component of a larger institution may be separately accreditable if a significant portion of responsibility and decision making for its educational activities lies within the component and not in the other parts of the larger system" (North Central Association of Colleges and Schools, Commission on Institutions of Higher Education, 1992, p. 49). The handbook explicitly notes that determination of a component's separate status and of site visit conduct depends entirely on consultation between the system's chief executive officer and the commission.

Northwest Association of Schools and Colleges, Commission on Colleges. As noted in its *Accreditation Handbook* (1992), the Northwest Association of Schools and Colleges Commission on Colleges follows the general FRACHE guidelines for defining an operationally separate unit, including operation under a parent institution, a core of full-time faculty, a separate student body, and a resident administration. Decisions about the separate accreditation of operationally separate units rest with the accrediting commission. In consultation with the institution, the commission arranges the manner in which the evaluation will be carried out and accreditation designated.

Southern Association of Colleges and Schools, Commission on Colleges. Like North Central's policy, the policy of the Southern Association of Colleges and Schools' Commission on Colleges (1992, 1990a) toward branch campus accreditation depends on institutional negotiation with the commission. The commission requires individual units to apply for separate accreditation when they meet commission criteria that permit individual compliance with accreditation requirements and the institution requests accreditation, or when the commission determines "the unit has achieved ... [a significant] level of autonomy" (Southern Association of Colleges and Schools, Commission on Colleges, 1991, pp. 28–29; 1990a, p. 1; 1990b, p. 1).

Western Association of Schools and Colleges, Accrediting Commission for Senior Colleges and Universities. The Western Association of Schools and Colleges' Accrediting Commission for Senior Colleges and Universities (1988) depends to a slightly lesser extent on the original FRACHE definitions, adding some caveats to the usual criteria for units that can be separately accredited. The commission reserves the right to interpret its definition of separate units, but also makes the general statement that operationally separate units require separate accreditation. The commission also provides accreditation process guidelines that focus on the efficacy of system administration to a greater extent than called for by other regional commissions.

Commission Interpretation and Application of Guidelines to Branch Campuses

We surveyed accreditation commission representatives by telephone, using fixed key questions. The respondents represented all six regional accrediting commissions and included two executive directors, three associate directors, and one deputy director. Although the key questions directed the survey, conversations often took interesting turns.

Key Questions. Key questions were asked about site definition, multisite accreditation policy development, the multisite accreditation process, the relationship between government and accreditation, and the effectiveness of current policies and practices. For example, we asked, By what criteria does the commission define a site? What policies and practices affect the eventual decision about site dependency or autonomy? How did branch campus accreditation policy and practice develop? What historical influences guided the development? What factors account for variation among associations? Will this variation continue or is greater uniformity anticipated? What is the process for multisite branch campus accreditation? What determines site visits and evaluation team membership for branch campuses? How have government regulations or initiatives affected branch campus accreditation policies and practices? How will the thrust for greater accountability arising from government influence future policy and practice? How satisfied are the associations and their membership with current policies and practices? What determines satisfaction or dissatisfaction? In cases of dissatisfaction, what remedial action, if any, suggests itself?

Amplification of Written Policy. Four of the six commission representatives responded that their written policy provided only partial information about actual policy and procedure. Those that amplify written policies intimated that their commission documents represent only guidelines for actual practice and that criteria employed to determine an educational unit's independence often exceed written guidelines, depending more on negotiation and evaluators' judgment than policy statements. One commission, for example, reported using additional informal criteria developed from the students' perspective, such as whether a student's ability to take the bulk of course credit for graduation at a particular site justifies calling that site a separately accreditable unit. Two other commissions said directly that they did not use their written policy much because it did not sufficiently delineate central as opposed to shared or diffuse control, a distinction that determined whether a specific site should be accredited separately.

Principal Influences on Policy Development. Most respondents agreed that their policy emanated from the FRACHE guidelines of the early 1970s. However, two commissions had no current staff who had been with their commission long enough to recall the historical development of existing policy and procedures. Two other commissions have moved well beyond the FRACHE document, and the two remaining appear to continue to use it as a foundation for present action. In short, FRACHE appears to have provided the initial definition of operationally separate units; however, each of the regions has since gone its own way in interpreting and applying that definition.

Impetus for Policy Change. The impetus for and scope of policy change varied. One commission had reformed its policy in order to focus on evaluators' determination of a campus's control locus, after evaluation teams visiting campuses could not get clear answers about the locus of authority. As a result, this commission now accredits fewer individual sites in multisite systems. Another respondent described a formal process for changing commission policy, which focused on developing criteria for the determination of site dependence or independence. Only one respondent described an external force—in this case, accountability to the federal government—as the stimulus for policy review and revision. Clearly, different commissions have had different motivations for change. And even though the change stimuli may originally have had some common elements, the net result is divergence in the ways the commissions determine branch campuses' autonomy.

Process of Policy Determination. The process that led to development of a separate-site policy also varied. However, all respondents reported relatively or totally noncontentious policy development processes. Most commissions relied on staff-initiated policy suggestions arising from difficulties encountered in the field with multisite evaluation. Considering the variations in the policies the commissions developed, the descriptions of nonfractious definition processes may say more about preferred working styles and individual regional association cultures than about the policies themselves. At the same time, several respondents volunteered that, even though policy development was not contentious, site definition has become increasingly problematic, especially in terms of off-campus and international activity. Commission spokespeople cited a number of variables that had to be considered, including academic governance and academic quality at separate sites, and problems deriving from delivering programs over a distance. As differences in commission criteria for defining and reviewing a site other than the parent campus suggest, commission specificity about what characterizes a separate unit diverges markedly. Some commissions have no criteria and rely on negotiation while others have criteria of varying degrees of formality.

Branch Campus Self-Study and Site Visits. Predictably, accrediting commissions with more specific site definitions also have more specific self-study and site visit policies and practices. However, taken as a group, commission requirements for self-study and site visits range from the totally idiosyncratic and individually negotiated to the precisely specified in advance. Some commission respondents said that they generally try to visit each site, others that the issue was not a matter of negotiation. Some said that since they accredited the whole institution, all parts had better be involved; others said that they required a detailed self-study from each unit of a multisite institution.

State Influence on Accreditation and Branch Campuses. State regulations appear to have very limited influence on either general accreditation practices or those specific to branch campuses. Some states require accreditation for licensure and may or may not participate in accreditation visits.

Although a state's definition of a separate site may differ from that of an accrediting commission's, the commission's prevails in all cases for the purposes of accreditation.

Public Policy Issues

To those concerned about the broad public policy issues that surround the accrediting of two-year institutions, issues articulated by Palinchak in Chapter One, our analysis of the regional accrediting commissions' various positions regarding two-year branch campuses of four-year universities provides little comfort. None of the six accreditors appears to view these campuses as having special attributes along the lines described in Chapter One and, therefore, perhaps deserving accreditation considerations different from those used to evaluate a system's central campus. There is no explicit recognition that the commissions' typical measures of academic excellence should vary for two-year institutions that have missions that are different from those of the much larger, overarching colleges or from the universities within which the two-year schools are embedded. Although each commission evaluates institutional effectiveness in achieving self-defined goals and outcomes as well as in meeting commission standards, none requires individual campus explication and goal assessment. Individual assessment might occur, but since the evaluation process may rely on site sampling or negotiation about site selection, no assurance exists that each campus has set and met goal expectations.

Two-year branch campuses typically have divergent goals and priorities from their parent institutions, with greater emphasis on teaching and much less emphasis on research and scholarship. In addition, two-year branch campuses tend to be vehicles for delivering associate degrees that are expected to result in immediate employment. Two-year branch campus practitioners often confront conflicts arising from having a purpose and population different from that of the larger institution; yet umbrella assessment of the entire system assumes that the various campuses have homogeneous missions and goals. And what does it say about accreditation's validity if a two-year campus in one region achieves accreditation after an individual self-study and external team visit but a similar two-year campus in another region achieves its status as a result of a global institutional accreditation? Does direct accreditation confer greater stature on one than the other? Has one profited more than the other by being actively involved with an internal and external review process?

Implications for the Future

The fact that regional commissions differ so much in their treatment of branch campuses does not bode well for the intercommission, interregional cooperation that assessment of cross-boundary, cross-border education at distant sites increasingly will require. Two-year campuses are only one stop on the ever-growing continuum of higher education sites made available through ever more sophisticated instructional technologies. And two-year campuses are arguably an easier stop to bypass than those that lie ahead. Therefore, at this point, it would probably be counterproductive to focus only on individual evaluations or specific criteria for two-year branch campuses for the purposes of accreditation. Rather, accrediting associations and their member institutions must face the more formidable task of redefining and measuring educational excellence within many diverse settings, of which branch campuses are only one example.

Although in the past commission-institutional negotiation has been a relatively nonfractious process for determining what constitutes a site, this approach may not serve as well in a future of far more complex interregional and international delivery systems. The number of interested parties will likely increase exponentially, making negotiation or political resolution much less feasible and certainly less acceptable to the public and government. A more proactive, more coordinated interregional approach to reviewing and evaluating extensions of collegiate education seems imperative for continued public confidence in accreditation. The criteria used to determine excellence in multisited institutions require a significant shift of emphasis. Accreditation will have to focus more on output than input and more on procedural than descriptive characteristics.

References

Middle States Association of Colleges and Schools, Commission on Higher Education. *Accreditation, Special Programs, Off-Campus Educational Activities and New Degree Levels.* Philadelphia: Middle States Association of Colleges and Schools, 1984.

Middle States Association of Colleges and Schools, Commission on Higher Education. *Characteristics of Excellence.* Philadelphia: Middle States Association of Colleges and Schools, 1990.

Middle States Association of Colleges and Schools, Commission on Higher Education. *Evaluation of Multi-Unit Institutions.* Philadelphia: Middle States Association of Colleges and Schools, 1991a.

Middle States Association of Colleges and Schools, Commission on Higher Education. *Separate Accreditation of Units Within Multi-Unit Institutions.* Philadelphia: Middle States Association of Colleges and Schools, 1991b.

Middle States Association of Colleges and Schools, Commission on Higher Education. *Separate Off-Campus Offerings: Handbook for Evaluators and Institutions.* Philadelphia: Middle States Association of Colleges and Schools, 1991c.

New England Association of Schools and Colleges, Commission on Institutions of Higher Education. *Operationally Separate Units.* Winchester, Mass.: New England Association of Schools and Colleges, 1972.

New England Association of Schools and Colleges, Commission on Institutions of Higher Education. *Standards for Accreditation, 1992.* Winchester, Mass.: New England Association of Schools and Colleges, 1992.

North Central Association of Colleges and Schools, Commission on Institutions of Higher Education. *A Handbook of Accreditation: 1992–93.* Chicago: North Central Association of Colleges and Schools, 1992.

Northwest Association of Schools and Colleges, Commission on Colleges. *Accreditation Handbook: 1992 Edition.* Seattle: Northwest Association of Schools and Colleges, 1992.

Southern Association of Colleges and Schools, Commission on Colleges. *The Accreditation of a Separate Unit.* Decatur, Ga.: Southern Association of Colleges and Schools, 1990a.

Southern Association of Colleges and Schools, Commission on Colleges. *Centers, Branches, Campuses, Extended Locations and Separate Units.* Decatur, Ga.: Southern Association of Colleges and Schools, 1990b.

Southern Association of Colleges and Schools, Commission on Colleges. *Policies, Procedures, and Guidelines of the Commission on Colleges: 1992–1993.* Decatur, Ga.: Southern Association of Colleges and Schools, 1991.

Southern Association of Colleges and Schools, Commission on Colleges. *Criteria for Accreditation.* Decatur, Ga.: Southern Association of Colleges and Schools, 1992.

Thrash, P. A. "Monitoring Educational Change: Evaluating Institutions with Off-Campus Programs." *North Central Association Quarterly,* 1979, 53 (3), 367–376.

Western Association of Schools and Colleges, Accrediting Commission for Senior Colleges and Universities. *Handbook of Accreditation.* Oakland, Calif.: Western Association of Schools and Colleges, 1988.

CORRINNE A. CALDWELL is campus executive officer of the Mont Alto Campus of The Pennsylvania State University.

LAWRENCE S. COTE is center executive officer of the Great Valley Center of The Pennsylvania State University, Malvern, Pennsylvania.

Although accrediting agencies permit two-year colleges to reform general education more than is sometimes assumed, these agencies can do more to encourage general learning.

The Role of Accreditation and General Education in Career Curricula

Carolyn Prager

What educators commonly call general education has been a focus for public discussion of higher education since the 1980s. From Bennett's *To Reclaim a Legacy* (1984) and the Association of American Colleges' *Integrity in the College Curriculum* (1985) to Boyer's *College: The Undergraduate Experience in America* (1987), national reports have assailed the erosion of liberal learning and the lack of curricular cohesion on U.S. campuses. These documents scrutinize perceived general education deficiencies in baccalaureate education. However, recognizing the argument's intrinsic importance for the associate degree, the American Association of Community and Junior Colleges (1992c) in 1986 called on all leaders of two-year institutions to examine the Bennett report for its relevance to their institutions. Today, there is another public imperative for educators. It is to meet National Education Goal number five, which calls for a level of U.S. adult literacy, knowledge, and skills by the year 2000 that will assure U.S. global competitiveness. In 1992, a National Education Goals Panel committee recommended development of a "sample-based national system of standards and assessment for postsecondary education" to measure "general cognitive skills, higher order thinking skills, and occupational specific skills where appropriate" (cited by Zook, 1993, p. A23). At the time of the writing of this chapter, the National Center for Educational Statistics had issued a request for contract proposals to develop the required measurement instrument.

These and other external forces at state and federal levels are enough to suggest that educational accountability will soon require educational institutions to move beyond the present system whereby accrediting bodies review and validate institutional self-study based on self-determined standards and self-assessed outcomes. With or without the imposition of state or national standards for general cognitive and higher order thinking skills, two-year colleges cannot ignore that part of the national debate about the country's educational preparedness for economic survival that calls for more substantive attention to general learning. At the same time, accrediting agencies cannot afford to be viewed as part of the problem and not of the solution.

Accreditation and Two-Year General Education

Criticism of the general education requirements for the associate degree tends to reflect the values of two distinct groups: those who believe the two-year educational sector's primary mission is to prepare students for employment and those who believe that mission is to prepare students for transfer to four-year colleges. The division of responsibilities for institutional and programmatic review between regional and specialized accrediting bodies is also related to the absence of a unified vision for two-year education. Under the current dualistic system of accreditation, if regional and specialized accreditors look at general education on a two-year campus at all, they have divergent perspectives. And when it comes to general education, specialized accrediting agencies are more often sinners of omission than commission.

Despite the importance given to general learning in public policy discussions about college outcomes, accrediting agencies have done little to help two-year institutions undertake new general education initiatives. As Peter Ewell puts it, "the assessment mechanisms that are best suited to demonstrating effectiveness are not always those that are the most helpful in the long run for program improvement" (1992, p. 10). By cultivating institutional outcomes assessment as the response to external demands for accountability, regional accreditors have sidestepped more fundamental questions such as how to make vocational study more academic. In the meantime, programmatic accreditors have, as a rule, either ignored general education entirely or addressed it by imposing limited distribution requirements. How can peer and professional review agencies do more to help two-year schools rethink general education for associate degrees that prepare people for employment, for transfer, and often for both?

Specialized Accreditation

Two-year colleges are intensely involved in specialized programmatic accreditation. Between 1980 and 1992, the number of programmatic approval bodies recognized by the Council on Postsecondary Accreditation increased from thirty-nine to forty-three. One of these, the Committee on Allied Health Education and Accreditation (CAHEA), itself sponsors nineteen professional organizations responsible for allied health program review. As documented by Kells and Parrish (1986), the specialized accreditation of career-oriented programs at two-year regionally approved institutions contributed substantially to the overall increase in accreditation activity between 1978 and 1985. According to an American Council on Education (ACE) survey, two-year campuses reported an average of three visits each by specialized accreditors between 1983 and 1986, compared to two each for baccalaureate institutions. Two-year institutions also had an average of five accredited programs on campus compared to three at four-year schools in the same period (Anderson, 1987).

Campus Perceptions About Programmatic Accreditation and General Education. Historically, institutions of higher education have indicated that specialized accreditation has had a depressing effect on general education in vocational-technical curricula (see, for example, Messersmith and Medsker's 1969 study, especially pp. 58–61). Overall, colleges and universities appear to consider specialized accreditors somewhat more intrusive on a curriculum than regional associations and more restrictive in terms of general education (Anderson, 1987; Irvin, 1990; Simmons, 1988). Two-year colleges perceive more strongly than other higher education sectors that accreditors' influence over a curriculum hampers institutional attempts to review and revise general education goals and course distribution and delivery modes. In the ACE survey of accreditation issues, 35 percent of two-year respondents did *not* find that "specialized accreditation assures me that the standards and quality of my programs are generally acceptable in the postsecondary education community" (Anderson, 1987, p. 7). Nineteen percent of university and 27 percent of comprehensive and baccalaureate degree college representatives responded negatively to the same statement.

Of the twenty-four ACE survey questions about specialized accrediting, those pertaining to general education generated the most negative responses from all educational sectors. Forty-seven percent of two-year respondents believed that "course requirements make it difficult for the institution to achieve the breadth of knowledge it wants its graduates to have" (Anderson, 1987, p. 7), while 43 percent indicated that required course sequences were too prescriptive. Of 374 respondents, 73 percent at baccalaureate and 56 percent at associate degree institutions faulted programmatic accreditation because the "courses and course sequences required . . . limit the number of general education courses students can take" (p. 7).

Programmatic Accreditation Guidelines. Although some specialized accreditors mandate course and credit hour distribution in general and specialized areas, most prefer to list the technical competencies that institutions are expected to introduce into the curriculum in an organized fashion. The Accreditation Board for Engineering and Technology (1989), for example, still maintains minimum credit hour distribution requirements for technical, basic science and math, humanities, and social science courses in accreditable associate degree engineering technology programs.

However, the National League for Nursing (1991) has changed a former requirement that 40 percent of the curriculum be dedicated to general education. The league's 1991 criteria ask institutions only to provide a nonnursing course rationale that is consistent with the associate degree nursing program's philosophy and outcomes. Most of the allied health programs under the CAHEA umbrella prescribe little or no general education for the training of technicians, with the exception of basic science courses in some programs. Their program "essentials" speak primarily about the occupational competencies to be achieved within a framework of appropriately sequenced "units, modules, and/or courses" (Joint Review Committee for Respiratory Therapy Education, p. IV-4, 1986), "content areas" (Joint Review Committee on Educational Programs in Nuclear Medicine Technology, 1991, p. 9), or "subject areas (which do not necessarily imply individual courses)" (Joint Review Committee for the Ophthalmic Medical Assistant, 1988, p. 3), to cite three specific examples.

However written, such guidelines do not appear to overtly restrict two-year institutions from rethinking the share of general education in their programs, whether through increasing arts and sciences course requirements or through integrating general and career education. But it can be argued that the absence of a strong general education mandate in program guidelines does restrict attention to general education issues. This absence may also be grounds for the charge that accreditors do little to encourage integration of general and career education. In addition, accreditation obviously exerts influence through an "array of power brokers" (Simmons, 1988, p. 62) such as agency spokespeople and site evaluators as well as through written statements. Nonetheless, an actual reading of program accreditation policies and guidelines suggests strongly that, in the eyes of the accreditors, decisions about what is taught and where and how it is taught reside mainly with the educational institutions, and most specialized accreditation guidelines exhibit considerable tolerance for colleges' packaging technical competencies in ways that theoretically permit whatever arts and sciences credit hour allocations the colleges deem necessary. Therefore, campus academic leaders can foster more informed discussion with faculty and outside evaluators by becoming better versed in program accreditation specifics and the latitude allowed for general education coursework and integration. Paying attention to how accreditation guidelines are interpreted and who interprets them may be critical to assuring that career programs reflect, endorse, and sustain an institution's general education philosophy and design.

Divergent Voices Urge General Education Reform

Saying that accreditation agencies may not actively hinder colleges from restructuring general education to the extent these agencies are sometimes thought to do is not the same as saying that they actively help two-year campuses resolve different views about the value of general learning stemming from inherent mission dualities and heterogeneous interest groups. The emergence of vocational curricula, each with its detailed set of occupational proficiencies, has led to the concept that the major in U.S. higher education is dominated by technical rather than liberal learning. Before the publication of Bennett's *To Reclaim a Legacy*, Conrad (1983) had already described a decline in the amount and scope of two-year college general education work during the previous fifteen years. By the early 1980s, for example, most community colleges had dropped such rigorous science and humanities requirements as college mathematics and foreign languages and had liberalized student choices within required areas of career and, sometimes, transfer programs.

Through the sheer weight of their enrollments, occupational-technical programs have probably had a greater effect on general learning at associate degree than at baccalaureate institutions. Also, many different voices speak for different kinds of general education at two-year schools, in ways that complicate that education's needed reconceptualization. The politics of two-year colleges dictate attention to the often conflicting concerns of such divergent groups as employers, students, faculty, government, the two-year sector as a whole, and higher education at large.

Employers and General Education. Most community colleges have abandoned the traditional university model of humanistic education as a coherent intellectual experience in favor of a model that conceives of general education in terms of derivative skills such as writing and speaking (Conrad, 1983; Richardson, Fisk, and Okum, 1983; Cohen and Brawer, 1987). This revised view of the liberal arts (and, to a lesser extent, the sciences) from intellectual and fundamental to pragmatic but peripheral has lessened the perceived necessity for in-depth liberal arts study. As Cohen and Brawer put it, "the result is that the liberal arts in community colleges hardly resemble the contemplative, text-centered courses that are posed as the ideal in the university" (1987, p. 171).

Numerous studies document that employers usually rank such specific general education skills as writing, speaking, and thinking of greater importance for employment than occupational-technical courses (see Nolte, 1991, for a useful review of representative studies). On the rare occasions when employers have been asked where or how these general education skills should be taught, the judgments of these business and industry representatives differ little from those made by educators. The employers see the desired skills as the natural outcome of particular courses in English, mathematics, computer literacy, and economics, as opposed to study in philosophy or fine arts, and the employers would devote about 30 percent of the two-year career curriculum to such subjects (Meyer, 1983; Perkins, 1985; Armistead, Lemon, Perkins, and Armistead, 1989).

General approaches to problem evaluation and solving can be taught within most any discipline, and the general education outcomes employers say they want could probably be cultivated within vocational courses were these courses to be taught differently. However, leaving that idea aside for the moment, a discrepancy still exists between the value put on skills believed to derive from general education coursework and the amount of time employers and educators would dedicate to these classes in career curricula. How then are these desired skills to be achieved?

Students and General Education. Though more limited in number than employer surveys, surveys of occupational-technical completers and leavers indicate that current and former students also place greater importance on English, mathematics, and economics than on the natural sciences, fine arts, and like subjects, which are seen as less job related. Rather universally, career students tend to believe that their programs contain too much general education. Reflecting the student viewpoint, Armistead, Moore, and Vogler (1987) (see also Armistead and Vogler, 1987; Vogler and Armistead, 1987; Armistead, Lemon, Perkins, and Armistead, 1989) recommend that occupational-technical programs diminish attention to general education courses and competencies deemed less important by students. Moreover, they recommend that vocational curricula suit mathematics requirements to the degree program and broaden student choice among general education courses.

Community College Critics and General Education. For more than a quarter of a century, community college critics have deplored the decline in quality and quantity of two-year transfers to four-year programs (see, for example, Brint and Karabel, 1989). From the critics' perspective, community college attendance in itself reduces the likelihood that two-year students will aspire to or complete the baccalaureate. Among the major explanations the critics give for community colleges' negative effect are the increasing numbers of students electing vocational majors in two-year institutions, the decreasing emphasis on the liberal arts and sciences in all majors but especially occupational-technical ones, and the declining academic rigor of occupational-technical courses.

The Community College Sector and General Education Reform

The policy statements of the American Association of Community and Junior Colleges (AACJC) reflect the sometimes fractious debates about the nature, value, and distribution of associate degree general education. In response to general public criticism of higher education, the association adopted a consensus document in 1984 calling for associate degree education that pays "full attention . . . to continuity in learning, as well as to the proficiencies required for an individual to achieve career understanding."

This education requires a "coherent and tightly knit sequence of courses" (American Association of Community and Junior Colleges, 1992a, p. 158). In 1986, the AACJC recommended that colleges limit Associate in Applied Science (A.A.S.) technical specialty courses to no more than 50 to 75 percent of course credits (American Association of Community and Junior Colleges, 1992b, p. 163). While the recommendation is commendable in its overall intent, setting a minimum standard of 25 percent for general education coursework simply approximates the reality for general education in most existing community and technical college vocational programs and hardly addresses the concerns of those who argue for a more liberally educated A.A.S. graduate.

In 1986, the AACJC also issued a policy statement advocating attention to the humanities in every community college degree program and establishing minimums for humanities coursework ranging from six semester hours for the Associate in Applied Science to twelve for the Associate in Arts. While the statement acknowledges that the "humanities do have inherent worth," it devotes considerably more discussion to the "practical" benefits of humanistic pursuits (American Association of Community and Junior Colleges, 1992c, p. 168).

The Accreditation Community and General Education Reform

While the ferment has raged about the quality of U.S. undergraduate education, the accreditation community has been strangely silent about the part it has played and could play in improving educational quality. The idea of accreditation as a potential change agent is conspicuously absent in the series of national reports on the baccalaureate (Wolff, 1990). Until recently, the notion of accreditation as a change agent has been absent as well from the two-year sector's multifaceted discussions about ways to improve two-year education and general learning outcomes.

Articulation and Transfer. Due to increased public interest in community college student progression to the baccalaureate, some commentators have begun to question the accrediting community's commitment to transfer and articulation, and have implied and suggested influential roles accrediting agencies might assume in guiding academic development that leads to transfer (see, for example, Knoell, 1990, p. 60; American Council on Education, 1991; Prager, 1992). To the extent that accrediting agencies are really quasi-public bodies working in lieu of governmental agencies to assure the larger community about educational accountability, regional accreditors are "uniquely positioned to create demanding expectations of institutional transfer activity" (American Council on Education, 1991, p. 6).

The same might be said of specialized accreditors. They have the potential to set requirements for good faith efforts by both four- and two-year institutions to achieve either downward or upward program articulation, as the case may be. They also have the potential to set related requirements for the development of programs that will enable associate degree career students to move more seamlessly onto the baccalaureate track with the general education abilities needed to succeed in upper-level work (Prager, 1992).

Accreditation and Career Faculty Credentials. Some accrediting bodies require two- or four-year technical faculty to have a baccalaureate degree, but some require only an associate degree, and some require no formal college education. The varying educational requirements listed above are found especially in allied health areas (Prager, 1992). Yet it is reasonable to assume a correlation between faculties' educational attainment and their commitment to promoting similar educational goals and values in students. It is also reasonable to assume that faculties' formal education in the larger historical, social, economic, and other cultural contexts of their respective professions will lead them to appreciate the cultivation of similar understandings in their students. By setting higher academic standards for specialized program faculty at two-year undergraduate institutions, accrediting bodies could foster a better climate for discussion of general education's role in career curricula.

Accreditation and General Education Integration of Career Curricula. The assumption that arts and sciences study is good for students primarily because it helps them to think and better express themselves creates several problems for those who seek more cohesive and balanced career curricula. First, the premium put on the practical feeds the notion that arts and sciences lack intrinsic value and thus need not be studied in any organized fashion. Second, the emphasis on the practical ignores the extent to which intensive study of abstract concepts contributes to a greater capacity for thoughtful application in the arts, sciences, and technologies. Third, the assumption that study of arts and sciences is valid mainly because it improves communication and analytical dexterity ignores the possibility that these essential skills can be taught in other study contexts, and relieves the occupational-technical teacher from most responsibility for reinforcing communication and analytical skills in career coursework. Fourth, the intellectual divide between technical and liberal studies in terms of anticipated academic outcomes deeply fragments the educational experience for both students and teachers.

What can regional and specialized accreditation bodies do to advance general education in career curricula and halt the further "degradation of academic culture" (McGrath and Spear, 1991, p. 63) in two-year education? They can do much to counteract the "ideology of neutral eclecticism [that] may now be the biggest obstacle to curricular reform" (McGrath and Spear, 1991, p. 63) by attending as much to the general as to the occupational competencies required of graduates. This means working with other accrediting bodies and the educational institutions to rethink not only why general education should be an integral part of career education but also how the integration can be realized. Successful models integrating humanistic and applied education do exist, many from four-year institutions (see, for example, the work of the Professional Preparation Network, explored throughout Armour and Fuhrmann, 1989). Accrediting associations and associate degree–granting schools could use these models as an objective base for fruitful discussion about ways to encourage a unified vision of two-year schooling and endow vocational programs with more of the strengths traditionally said to derive from liberal study.

Supported by a grant from the Fund for the Improvement of Postsecondary Education, the Shared Vision Task Force of the National Council for Occupational Education and the Community College Humanities Association have developed several possibilities for integrating the humanities in career programs (Community College Humanities Association, 1991). The possibilities include revision of particular humanities and occupational courses, combination of revised humanities and occupational courses into a new humanities course, and development of a new interdisciplinary hybrid course, among others. The Shared Vision Task Force has funded various projects for integrating humanities and occupational courses at Clackamas, Seminole, and Eastern Iowa Community Colleges, as well as Southern Maine Technical Institute. Concerned about its "cafeteria" approach to the humanities, Kirkwood Community College secured a National Endowment for the Humanities grant to create three interdisciplinary humanities courses on topics of special interest to career students. The courses are *Working in America, Technology and the Human Condition,* and *Living in the Information Age* (Eisenberg, Gollattscheck, Metcalf, and Shapiro, 1991).

Responding to calls for a change from a technical to a more broad-based education, the Accounting Education Change Commission awarded project grants to Kirkwood and Mesa Community Colleges for the academic year 1991–92 (Ernst and Young, 1992). Kirkwood's project was to revise a two-semester principles of accounting course so that it would help students improve their communication and critical thinking skills, knowledge of the business environment's influence on accounting, and grasp of accounting concepts. The revision led to a reduced emphasis on the procedural aspects of accounting and an increased emphasis on changing accounting instructors' teaching methods. Mesa's project was to achieve similar course goals through extensive use of case studies to illustrate and analyze significant accounting and business concepts. Such projects extend general education into career curricula in two ways: first, through increased attention to general education skills and applications that are to be acquired in greater breadth across an entire curriculum, including technical courses; and second, through increased attention to general education knowledge and understanding acquired in greater depth through better structured, more intensive humanities and interdisciplinary coursework.

Call for Coordinated Accreditation Policies and Practices

Theoretically and practically, today's regional accreditors focus on outcomes assessment, concerning themselves with overall institutional approaches to general education. Under prevailing conditions, programmatic accrediting agencies may or may not review the general education coursework or skills an institution incorporates into its specialized degree tracks. Both forms of accreditation have great potential to help two-year colleges respond to current pressures from within and without to improve the academic background and abilities of career and transfer students. Achieving this potential, however, requires accreditors and institutions to develop a unified vision of associate degree education, whether for transfer, for employment, or for both.

Regional and specialized accreditors can encourage more complex engagement with the liberal arts and sciences by requiring evidence of orderly and incremental arts and sciences study in reviews of career and transfer programs. Accreditors can also encourage attention to such academic skills and abilities as writing and problem solving by requiring institutions to document the skills' reinforcement and integration in technical as well as arts and sciences coursework. Like the institutions they serve, accreditors can best do this by coordinating their attention to general education needs and consciously bridging the distance between the two cultures of general and technical studies, a distance for which separate regional and specialized accreditation bears some responsibility.

References

Accreditation Board for Engineering and Technology. *Criteria for Accrediting Programs in Engineering Technology: Effective for Evaluations During the 1990–1991 Academic Year.* New York: Accreditation Board for Engineering Technology, 1989.

American Association of Community and Junior Colleges. "Policy Statement on the Associate Degree." In *AACJC Membership Directory 1992.* Washington, D.C.: American Association of Community and Junior Colleges, 1992a.

American Association of Community and Junior Colleges. "Policy Statement on the Associate of Applied Science Degree." In *AACJC Membership Directory 1992.* Washington, D.C.: American Association of Community and Junior Colleges, 1992b.

American Association of Community and Junior Colleges. "Policy Statement on the Humanities." In *AACJC Membership Directory 1992.* Washington, D.C.: American Association of Community and Junior Colleges, 1992c.

American Council on Education National Center for Academic Achievement and Transfer. *Setting the National Agenda: Academic Achievement and Transfer: A Policy Statement and Background Paper About Transfer Education.* Washington, D.C.: American Council on Education, 1991.

Anderson, C. J. *Survey of Accreditation Issues: 1986*. Higher Education Panel Report, no. 74. Washington, D.C.: American Council on Education, 1987. 47 pp. (ED 283 427)

Armistead, L. P., Lemon, J., Perkins, D. R., and Armistead, J. S. "The Amount and Importance of General Education in the Two-Year Occupational Curriculum According to Corporate Employers." *Community/Junior College Quarterly of Research and Practice*, 1989, *13* (2), 91–99.

Armistead, L. P., Moore, D. M., and Vogler, D. E. "Selected General Education Influences Affecting Degree Completion for Community College Occupational Students." *Community College Review*, 1987, *15* (3), 55–59.

Armistead, L. P., and Vogler, D. E. "Actual and Optimal Amounts of General Education in Occupational Programs." *Community/Junior College Quarterly of Research and Practice*, 1987, *11* (3), 153–162.

Armour, R. A., and Fuhrmann, B. S. (eds.). *Integrating Liberal Learning and Professional Education*. New Directions for Teaching and Learning, no. 40. San Francisco: Jossey-Bass, 1989.

Association of American Colleges. *Integrity in the College Curriculum: A Report to the Academic Community. The Findings and Recommendations of the Project on Redefining the Meaning and Purpose of Baccalaureate Degrees*. Washington, D.C.: Association of American Colleges, 1985. 62 pp. (ED 251 059)

Bennett, W. J. *To Reclaim a Legacy: A Report on the Humanities in Higher Education*. Washington, D.C.: National Endowment for the Humanities, 1984. 63 pp. (ED 247 880)

Boyer, E. L. *College: The Undergraduate Experience in America*. New York: HarperCollins, 1987.

Brint, S., and Karabel, J. *The Diverted Dream: Community Colleges and the Promise of Educational Opportunity in America, 1900–1985*. New York: Oxford University Press, 1989.

Cohen, A. M., and Brawer, F. B. *The Collegiate Function of Community Colleges: Fostering Higher Learning Through Curriculum and Student Transfer*. San Francisco: Jossey-Bass, 1987.

Community College Humanities Association. *Successfully Integrating the Humanities into Associate Degree Occupational Programs: An Implementation Manual*. Philadelphia: Community College Humanities Association, 1991.

Conrad, C. F. *At the Crossroads: General Education in Community Colleges*. Horizon Issues Monograph Series. Washington, D.C.: American Association of Community and Junior Colleges, 1983. 80 pp. (ED 229 090)

Eisenberg, D. U., Gollattscheck, J. F., Metcalf, D. H., and Shapiro, B. C. *Advancing Humanities Studies at Community, Technical, and Junior Colleges*. Washington, D.C.: American Association of Community and Junior Colleges, 1991.

Ernst and Young. *Update on Developments in Accounting Education*. A report by the accounting firm of Ernst and Young. New York: Ernst and Young, 1992.

Ewell, P. T. "Outcomes Assessment, Institutional Effectiveness, and Accreditation: A Conceptual Exploration." In *Accreditation, Assessment and Institutional Effectiveness: Resource Papers for the COPA Task Force on Institutional Effectiveness*. Washington, D.C.: Council on Postsecondary Accreditation, 1992.

Irvin, Glenn. "The Plight of General Education." *Educational Forum*, 1990, *54* (4), 371–387.

Joint Review Committee for Respiratory Therapy Education. *Essentials and Guidelines of an Accredited Educational Program for the Respiratory Therapy Technician and Respiratory Therapist*. Euless, Tex.: Joint Review Committee for Respiratory Therapy Education, 1986.

Joint Review Committee for the Ophthalmic Medical Assistant. *Essentials and Guidelines of an Accredited Educational Program for the Ophthalmic Medical Technician and Ophthalmic Medical Technologist*. St. Paul, Minn.: Joint Review Committee for the Ophthalmic Medical Assistant, 1988.

Joint Review Committee on Educational Programs in Nuclear Medical Technology. *Essentials and Guidelines for an Accredited Educational Program for the Nuclear Medicine Technologist*. Salt Lake City, Utah: Joint Review Committee on Educational Programs in Nuclear Medical Technology, 1991.

Kells, H. R., and Parrish, R. M. *Trends in the Accreditation Relationships of U.S. Postsecondary Institutions, 1978–1985.* Washington, D.C.: Council on Postsecondary Accreditation, 1986. 17 pp. (ED 297 684)

Knoell, D. M. *Transfer, Articulation, and Collaboration: Twenty-Five Years Later.* Washington, D.C.: American Association of Community and Junior Colleges, 1990. 109 pp. (ED 318 528)

McGrath, D., and Spear, M. B. *The Academic Crisis of the Community College.* Albany: State University of New York Press, 1991.

Messersmith, L. E., and Medsker, L. L. *Problems and Issues in Accreditation by Specialized Agencies of Vocational-Technical Curricula in Postsecondary Institutions.* Washington, D.C.: Office of Education, Cooperative Research Program, 1969.

Meyer, R. B. "Desired General Education Competencies: A Corporate Perspective." Unpublished doctoral dissertation, Virginia Polytechnic Institute and State University, 1983.

National League for Nursing. *Criteria and Guidelines for the Evaluation of Associate Degree Programs in Nursing.* (7th ed., rev.) New York: National League for Nursing, 1991.

Nolte, W. H. "Guaranteed Student Success: General Education and Occupational Programs." *Community College Review,* 1991, *19* (1), 14–23.

Perkins, D. R. "General Education Competencies as Outcomes of Two-Year Occupational Programs: A Comparison of Corporate and Academic Views." Unpublished doctoral dissertation, Virginia Polytechnic Institute and State University, 1985.

Prager, C. "Accreditation and Transfer: Mitigating Elitism." In B. W. Dziech and W. Vilter (eds.), *Prisoners of Elitism: The Community College's Struggle for Stature.* New Directions for Community Colleges, no. 78. San Francisco: Jossey-Bass, 1992.

Richardson, R. C., Jr., Fisk, E. A., and Okum, M. A. *Literacy in the Open-Admission College.* San Francisco: Jossey-Bass, 1983.

Simmons, H. "Accreditation and Curricular Change." In D. B. Wolf and M. L. Zoglin (eds.), *External Influences on the Curriculum.* New Directions for Community Colleges, no. 64. San Francisco: Jossey-Bass, 1988.

Vogler, D. E., and Armistead, L. P. "The Importance of General Education Courses and Competencies as Viewed by Community College Occupational Students." *Journal of Studies in Technical Careers,* 1987, *9* (3), 191–200.

Wolff, R. A. "Assessment and Accreditation: A Shotgun Marriage?" In *Assessment 1990: Accreditation and Renewal. Papers by Ralph A. Wolff and Alexander W. Astin Presented at the Fifth American Association for Higher Education Conference on Assessment in Higher Education.* Washington, D.C.: American Association for Higher Education, 1990.

Zook, J. "2 Agencies Start Work on National Test of College Students' Analytical Skills." *Chronicle of Higher Education,* Mar. 24, 1993, p. A23.

CAROLYN PRAGER *is dean of the College of Arts and Sciences at Franklin University, Columbus, Ohio.*

In an era of limited institutional resources, educators must reduce the
cost of accreditation while preserving its traditional benefits.

Cost-Benefit Analyses of Accreditation

Charles R. Reidlinger, Carolyn Prager

The expanding number of accrediting agencies and functions has intensified questions about their value. Do the number, frequency, and format of accrediting activities need closer scrutiny? Do accrediting agencies place realistic demands on institutions? Are these demands fiscally realistic or cost neutral? Are the benefits derived worth the efforts and revenue expended? These and similar questions related to cost have taken on a new urgency as discretionary resources diminish on many, if not most, of the nation's campuses.

Costs Versus Benefits

Previously, institutions of higher education had not aggressively pursued rigorous cost-based analyses of accreditation for at least two reasons. The first was a belief that cost was of secondary importance to the preservation of voluntary accreditation in lieu of involuntary government review—in other words, accreditation at any price was a benefit. The second reason was the methodological difficulty of relating accreditation's perceived benefits to real dollar costs. The fiscal environment of the 1990s, however, is driving many institutions to develop methods of relating accreditation's more easily measured costs to the less easily measured benefits. It appears also to be driving some institutions to selectively forgo accreditation.

There are many methodological problems in quantitatively assessing qualitative outcomes. Accreditation studies have generally looked at objective measures of costs and subjective perceptions of benefits, interpreting both costs and benefits loosely, with little common definition. Consequently, approaches that appear similar may lead to very different conclusions. From comparable data about accreditation, different analysts have concluded that benefits outweigh costs, benefits and costs balance, costs may outweigh benefits, or costs do outweigh benefits.

Benefits Outweigh Costs. Institutional and accrediting agency representatives who argue that accrediting benefits outweigh costs tend to measure value in reciprocal but different terms. A spokesperson for the accreditation community, on the one hand, is likely to appreciate the accreditation enterprise as "the primary means for effective self-regulation within the academic and professional communities," a regulation that would otherwise pass "by default" to state and federal governments (Millard, 1983, p. 36). From this vantage point, the benefits outbalance the costs, however determined. Institutional spokespeople, on the other hand, are much more likely to see accreditation's benefits as the processes of self-study and external review that help maintain or promote academic quality (see, for example, the surveys conducted by Yarbrough and Seymour [1985] and Anderson [1987]).

Benefits and Costs Balance. Chambers (1983) points out that the optimal balance justifying accreditation is between cost and social need. Through the 1970s, chief executive officers and those people Kells calls "the informed, relatively experienced minority" on campus (1983, p. 109) repeatedly defended the costs of accreditation on the basis of its institutional benefits, especially the self-study component. In these early studies, even when educators perceived accreditation expenses to be a burden, they agreed for the most part that the burden was not a serious issue compared to the important institutional gains (Pigge, 1979; Glidden, 1983).

Costs May Outweigh Benefits. As accrediting bodies and visits have proliferated, two-year campuses in particular have had reason to question accreditation's price and value. Anderson's national survey of accreditation issues (1987) reveals a shift away from the more universal endorsement of accreditation that Pigge and Kells had noted. In 1986, the nation's campuses offered approximately 13,600 programs accredited by specialized agencies, and more than 5,000 of these programs were at two-year campuses (Anderson, 1987, pp. vi, 7). In the three years prior to 1986, nearly 7,700 visits to examine programs had been made by specialized accrediting agencies alone (Anderson, 1987, p. vi). In 1986, only three-quarters of responding institutions agreed that specialized accreditation was a useful measure of program quality. Seventy-eight percent of baccalaureate colleges agreed this was so compared to only 68 percent of two-year schools (Anderson, 1987, p. 7). A larger percentage of the two-year sector than of other sectors doubted specialized accreditation's ability to measure program quality.

The survey revealed other interesting differences between two- and four-year degree-granting institutions. For example, while two-fifths of all respondents agreed that institutional accreditation precluded the need for specialized accreditation, more than one-half of the two-year colleges took this position. Thirty-six percent overall indicated that specialized accreditation was a source of low-cost consultation, but only 31 percent of the two-year schools said so. Twenty-two percent of all respondents said accreditation occurred too frequently, but 27 percent of two-year respondents felt this way. And 34 percent overall felt the dollar cost of specialized accreditation was too great, but 38 percent of two-year institutions believed this to be true (Anderson, 1987, p. 7).

Although the sectors' perceptions were not vastly different, two-year institutions had slightly greater reservations about accreditation's worth than did their senior counterparts for almost every cost-related item the survey queried. Why? We speculate that this occurred because two-year institutions make greater use than other institutions of additional assessment indices such as local advisory boards and external program reviews, which generate additional accreditation costs. The reason for the difference between sectors is outside the immediate scope of this essay, but we suggest that it merits further study.

Costs Do Outweigh Benefits. In its 1983 policy statement on specialized programmatic accreditation, the American Association of Community and Junior Colleges said that "colleges are beginning to seriously question whether programmatic accreditation improves the quality of education" (1992, p. 154). Indeed, some institutions have already decided that costs outweigh benefits and are acting accordingly by no longer participating in programmatic accreditation. Between 1983 and 1988, 736 programs withdrew from the Committee on Allied Health Education and Accreditation (CAHEA), the American Medical Association's umbrella agency for allied health review bodies (American Medical Association, 1992). The *Allied Health Education Directory* does not specify reasons for the programs' withdrawal, except to note that it was voluntary. Nonetheless, since CAHEA's inception in 1976, its agenda has included costing-related issues, which provide a context if not a specific explanation for the withdrawals. More explicitly, in severing connections with the National Council for Accreditation of Teacher Education, institutions such as the Universities of Arizona, Iowa, Northern Iowa, Arizona State University, and Northern Arizona State University explicitly pointed to the cost and time expended. Several teacher education programs have estimated costs to support accreditation activity of up to $300,000, for council membership fees, faculty and staff time, materials, and outlays for team site visits (Nicklin, 1992, pp. A19, A22).

Defining Cost

If cost is a critical component in an informed decision about accreditation's value, how should cost be defined? Obviously, cost has subjective as well as objective aspects. What one person may see as a cost, another may see as a benefit. This is the case, for example, when someone claims that an institution profits from the goodwill generated by a program even though maintaining the program requires monies that could otherwise be allocated to other worthy programs or institutional purposes. For accreditation, however, certain dollars-and-cents factors such as membership, self-study preparation, and site visit team support would seem to be available for building a cost data base to use when making decisions about value. Therefore, it is surprising how little agreement there seems to be about the possibility of determining accreditation's dollar costs, let alone what factors should be included in an accreditation cost data base. For example, in 1986, when CAHEA appointed a task force that was to form "recommendations leading to an overall systematic rational framework for the financing of all significant aspects of allied health program accreditation services" (American Medical Association, 1992, p. 9), the first of several problem areas the task force listed was the absence of current data about the costs of accreditation in dollars and in contributed services.

The accreditation literature reveals widely different assertions about accreditation costs with little in common except the reader's sense that everyone is counting by different rules. One writer suggests that the best institutions can do is generalize the direct cost of on-site visits for specialized accrediting bodies (Glidden, 1983). Other writers provide figures in the hundreds of thousands for accrediting a single program, as noted in the earlier examples of the teacher education programs. In 1981, the Association of Schools of Public Health surveyed twenty-two public health schools to obtain accreditation cost data. Total cost estimates ranged from $18,387 to $319,513 (Kennedy, Moore, and Thibadoux, 1985, p. 176). Kennedy, Moore, and Thibadoux comment that the differences in these reported costs were particularly interesting because the major program measure was the self-study, whose standardized format, procedures, and documentation requirements were prescribed in a manner that should have led to greater cost similarities between schools.

Other studies also show wide variations in amounts reported spent for similar accreditation functions in similar institutions (see, for example, Keyser, 1974; Yarbrough and Seymour, 1985). It seems evident that the variation occurs because the methods for defining and reporting costs vary (Kennedy, Moore, and Thibadoux, 1985). Thus, these methods affect judgments about accreditation's worth.

For example, Doerr's cost data (1983, pp. 6–8) from the accreditation visit of the National Council for Social Work to the University of West Florida in 1982 show costs in the categories of faculty time; secretarial time; supplies, materials, duplicating, and postage; professional services of a consultant; travel; and dues, reaching a total of $11,379 for the social work program's reaccreditation. Using the same cost elements, where they apply, Doerr arrives at a cost of $35,837 for the 1982 accreditation of the university's nursing program by the National League for Nursing. When other direct costs of the accreditation visit are added, the total is slightly over $50,000 expended in one year, without factoring in administrative time or sunk costs such as plant, equipment, depreciation, utilities, and so on. Kennedy, Moore, and Thibadoux (1985, p. 177), however, look at "opportunity costs" when calculating accreditation costs. That is, they calculate the value given up when resources are spent on accreditation rather than on other functions such as faculty research and curriculum development. In addition, when they look at self-study costs that are defined as cash outlays for materials and services consumed and time expended by faculty, administrative staff, and clerical personnel, they include computer time as a cash outlay and administrative time as time expended, elements not factored in by Doerr.

Toward a Common Methodology. Despite their variations, these methods and others do provide a starting point for institutions to identify the costs of the accrediting process in addition to membership dues and fees. Lenn (1987) breaks these costs into three categories. The first is a realistic institutional indirect cost rate. The second is actual material and services expenditures, including printing or photocopying, postage, and computer time. The third is actual payroll for time expended by administrators, faculty, consultants, and clerical staff. And there are probably additional categories. Lenn's list does not include such costs as faculty and staff travel to assessment and accreditation workshops and conferences and other costs that might represent considerable expense to certain schools. There are, for example, significant expenses to feed and house the accrediting team, whether these expenses are built into a prepaid membership or borne directly by the college, as discussed by Marti in Chapter Seven. To train institutional self-study leaders, New Mexico State University at Alamogordo, where one of the chapter authors serves as provost, has sent individuals to North Central Association accreditation meetings in Chicago for the past three years at a cost of $8,045. The methodological work to date, however, does provide a basis from which a group such as the National Association for College and University Business Officers could refine and define a standard for the determination of accreditation costs that could be employed by all institutions and agencies.

Relative Fiscal Impact. Given the frequency of complaints about cost, it is surprising how little information appears to exist about actual costs as a function of the total campus budget. Even more surprising is the absence of informed analysis of the effect of accreditation expenditures on different institutional types. Glidden (1983) posits that although cost is often cited as a major concern it probably is so only at larger schools, while Kells suggests that for "small institutions, even two or three accreditation relationships may be a burden" (1983, p. 110). Although he does not translate expenses into a percentage of campus operational costs, Doerr (1983, pp. 6–8) does project that two assistant professors could have been hired, several microcomputers purchased, or 2,500 books bought for the library with the

$50,000 spent on accreditation at the University of West Florida in 1982. This was at an institution that, at the time, enrolled about 5,500 students.

Using Lenn's categories (1987) and factoring in dues and memberships, we estimate that accreditation costs at the Alamogordo Campus for the past three years (including preparation for the 1993 North Central Association visit) have averaged 2.5 percent of the campus operating budget. This is for an institution with a head count of about 2,000, and 1,300 full-time equivalent students. Kennedy, Moore, and Thibadoux (1985, p. 182) estimate the 1982–83 accreditation costs at the University of Texas School of Public Health to be 1.5 percent of total expenditures from state-appropriated funds and 0.8 percent of total expenditures from all funding sources. In our judgment, the costs to Alamogordo are excessive; in Kennedy, Moore, and Thibadoux's judgment, the costs to the School of Public Health were not. Is this result merely a difference of opinion, or is there some relative threshold of tolerance that applies to differently configured and endowed institutions? Again, this is a topic with particular significance for two-year colleges, and one that we believe merits further inquiry.

In 1986, two-year colleges averaged five specialized programs per campus compared to seven for comprehensive institutions and fifteen for universities. However, the two-year schools that were surveyed had experienced a total of 2,798 visits in the three years prior to the survey, compared to only 1,676 visits for comprehensive schools and 1,030 for universities (Anderson, 1987, p. 15). We speculate that the higher figure for two-year schools resulted from some combination of new program development at the two-year schools and accreditation agency proliferation in the 1980s. According to Kells and Parrish (1986), there was an 81.2 percent volume increase in allied health education accreditations alone at regionally accredited institutions between 1978 and 1985. Of the ten agencies Kells and Parrish ranked highest in volume, four were involved in the evaluation of associate degree programs: the Accreditation Board for Engineering and Technology, the National League for Nursing, the Joint Review Committee for Education in Radiologic Technology, and the National Accrediting Agency for Clinical Laboratory Sciences. Whatever the reasons, two-year schools appear to have borne an inordinate share of the specialized accreditation burden, at least for the three years prior to 1986. If nothing else, these data suggest that more research needs to be done on the costs and fiscal impact of accreditation relative to different types and sizes of institutions.

Replacement Costs. Before rushing to judgment about the value of accreditation, institutions should examine accreditation expenses in relation to available resources and determine the replacement costs of accreditation benefits. In saying this, we bypass for the moment the argument that government abhors a vacuum and would seek to fill the lack of accreditation with its own set of expensive evaluative procedures. We argue instead that a college or university might still need to assess its programs and itself as an institution through self-studies and external reviews, for many of the reasons that gave rise to organized accreditation in the first place: to assure the public of qualitative outcomes, to qualify a program for state licensure, to improve programs, and so forth. In addition, institutions and programs would still seek natural affiliations with external professional bodies of like institutions and programs, and these affiliations have attendant costs. Given this scenario, institutions may find it more useful to seek ways to restrain accrediting costs than to forgo accreditation.

Institutional Role in Shaping Accreditation Costs and Benefits

In its 1983 position statement, the American Association of Community and Junior Colleges (AACJC) pointed to financial cost as one of three major institutional concerns about specialized programmatic accreditation. The proliferation of accrediting bodies and ensuing redundancy in what they look for and how they look at it has set the stage for reform of practice as well as policy. In 1981, the Council on Postsecondary Accreditation responded to this "inevitable duplication of efforts" (p. 1) by calling for more cooperation between accrediting agencies and more uniform and organized approaches to accreditation processes such as interagency coordinated visits, standards, and guidelines. In addition to describing institutional concerns about the cost, scope, and value of programmatic accreditation, the 1983 AACJC statement referred back to a policy that the AACJC had enunciated six years before and that addressed institutional practices and responsibilities such as becoming better informed about accreditation and reducing costs by seeking coordination of specialized and regional site visits. The New Hampshire Vocational-Technical College, for example, has developed a single self-study method for both institutional and program accreditation in an effort to increase the efficiency and lower the cost of this accreditation component (Stoodley, 1985).

The following list of recommendations for institutions concerned about containing costs and maximizing benefits is distilled from several sources (O'Neill and Heaney, 1982; Stoodley, 1983; Kells, 1983; Millard, 1984). The final item in the list is our own recommendation.

Develop greater awareness about the history, purposes, and scope of accreditation at the specific institution in order to better use future reviews to complement and advance institutional goals.
Appoint an accreditation officer to monitor accreditation activity nationally and regionally and to assist in planning and coordinating local accreditation reviews, rather than leave accreditation activity mainly to program faculty.
Develop a long-term accreditation plan as a basis for requesting coordinated

visits, for establishing data bases to be used across several reviews, and for spacing out visits and resources more evenly over several years.

Insist on joint or sequential reviews that maximize institutional goals and minimize costly redundancies between specialized agencies, between institutional and programmatic accreditors, and between governmental and accrediting agencies.

Monitor accreditation activity and use national associations to lobby aggressively for policies and practices judged to be beneficial and against those judged to be detrimental, including the formation of new accreditation commissions.

Conduct or call for comparative cost-based research that includes two-year colleges and provides all colleges and universities with common indicators with which to make informed judgments about the relative value of accreditation to the respective institution and the community it serves.

Preserving Benefits, Reducing Costs

Driven by increased costs and declining revenue, institutions of higher education are questioning segments of campus operations that they rarely examined closely before. On many campuses, accreditation is one of these questioned operations. Both the accreditors and the accredited should assume greater responsibility for reducing costs. As a first step, the accreditation community should acknowledge that cost is a concern that many institutions may no longer believe to be secondary to the preservation of self-regulation. For their part, colleges and universities should shape viable alternatives to the selective or blanket renunciation of accreditation by looking more thoughtfully at both accreditation's costs and its benefits.

References

American Association of Community and Junior Colleges. "AACJC Board Position on Specialized Programmatic Accreditation." In *AACJC Membership Directory 1992*. Washington, D.C.: American Association of Community and Junior Colleges, 1992.

American Medical Association. *Allied Health Education Directory 1992*. Chicago: American Medical Association, 1992.

Anderson, C. J. *Survey of Accreditation Issues 1986*. Higher Education Panel Report no. 74. Washington, D.C.: American Council on Education, 1987. 47 pp. (ED 283 427)

Chambers, C. M. "Characteristics of an Accrediting Body." In K. E. Young, C. M. Chambers, H. R. Kells, and Associates, *Understanding Accreditation: Contemporary Perspectives on Issues and Practices in Evaluating Educational Quality*. San Francisco: Jossey-Bass, 1983.

Council on Postsecondary Accreditation. *A Guide to Interagency Cooperation: Including Models of Successful Interagency Cooperative Efforts*. Washington, D.C.: Council on Postsecondary Accreditation, 1981.

Doerr, A. H. "Accreditation—Academic Boon or Bane?" *Contemporary Education*, 1983, 55 (1), 6–8.

Glidden, R. "Specialized Accreditation." In K. E. Young, C. M. Chambers, H. R. Kells, and Associates. *Understanding Accreditation: Contemporary Perspectives on Issues and Practices in Evaluating Educational Quality*. San Francisco: Jossey-Bass, 1983.

Kells, H. R. "Institutional Rights and Responsibilities." In K. E. Young, C. M. Chambers, H. R. Kells, and Associates, *Understanding Accreditation: Contemporary Perspectives on Issues and Practices in Evaluating Educational Quality*. San Francisco: Jossey-Bass, 1983.

Kells, H. R., and Parrish, R. M. *Trends in the Accreditation Relationships of U.S. Postsecondary Institutions, 1978–1985*. Washington, D.C.: Council on Postsecondary Education, 1986. 17 pp. (ED 297 684)

Kennedy, V. C., Moore, F. I., and Thibadoux, G. M. "Determining the Costs of Self-Study for Accreditation: A Method and a Rationale." *Journal of Allied Health*, 1985, *14* (2), 175–182.

Keyser, J. S. "An Evaluation of Specialized Regional and State Accrediting Activity in the Community Junior Colleges of the North Central Association Region." Unpublished doctoral dissertation, University of Colorado, 1974.

Lenn, M. P. "Accreditation, Certification, and Licensure." In M.A.F. Rehnke (ed.), *Creating Career Programs in a Liberal Arts Context*. New Directions for Higher Education, no. 57. San Francisco: Jossey-Bass, 1987.

Millard, R. M. "Accreditation, the Accrediting Association: Ensuring the Quality of Programs and Institutions." *Change*, 1983, *15* (4), 32–36.

Millard, R. M. "Whither Accreditation in the Health Professions?" *Educational Record*, 1984, *65* (4), 31–35.

Nicklin, J. L. "Teacher-Education Programs Debate the Need for Accrediting Agency's Stamp of Approval." *Chronicle of Higher Education*, May 6, 1992, pp. A19, A22.

O'Neill, T. M., and Heaney, R. P. "Taking the Initiative in Accreditation." *Educational Record*, 1982, *63* (4), 57–60.

Pigge, F. L. *Opinions About Accreditation and Interagency Cooperation: The Results of a Nationwide Survey of COPA Institutions*. Washington, D.C.: Council on Postsecondary Accreditation, 1979. 90 pp. (ED 177 944)

Stoodley, R. V., Jr. *Accrediting Occupational Training Programs*. Information Series no. 251. Columbus: National Center for Research in Vocational Education, Ohio State University, 1983. 89 pp. (ED 233 132)

Stoodley, R. V., Jr. *An Approach to Postsecondary Accreditation with the Efficient Use of Human Resources and Cost Containment Methods*. Unpublished paper by the president of New Hampshire Vocational-Technical College, 1985. 27 pp. (ED 271 150)

Yarbrough, M. M., and Seymour, J. C. "Regional Accreditation from the Two-Year Institutions' Perspective." *North Central Association Quarterly*, 1985, *59* (4), 37–77.

CHARLES R. REIDLINGER *is provost of New Mexico State University at Alamogordo.*

CAROLYN PRAGER *is dean of the College of Arts and Sciences at Franklin University, Columbus, Ohio.*

Institutional accreditation challenges the view that a community college is an open-ended institution with as many outcomes as there are students.

Institutional Accreditation, Student Outcomes Assessment, and the Open-Ended Institution

James C. Palmer

The process of institutional accreditation explores and validates an institution's overall purpose and capacity. When first introduced in the early decades of this century, accreditation primarily demanded that an institution meet minimum standards for library holdings, curricula, faculty, and other resources in order to satisfy the larger education community that an institution was what it claimed to be and had the wherewithal to teach students the knowledge and skills expected of those earning the institution's credentials. As the number and types of educational institutions grew in the mid–twentieth century, adherence to a common set of standards became impractical, and institutional self-studies came to the fore. Through these self-studies, schools validated their purpose and capacity by offering goals deemed appropriate for their type of enterprise, establishing processes for assessing degrees of goal attainment, and using assessment results for institutional improvement (Young, 1983; Bemis, 1983).

Contemporary accreditation procedures, influenced by the outcomes assessment movement (Ewell, 1992), retain the emphasis on self-study but add the requirement that college impacts on student learning and development be addressed. Though the wording of accreditation guidelines indicates variations between regional accrediting associations—for example, the North Central Association calls for assessments of "student academic achievement" (Mather, 1991) while the Southern Association of Colleges and Schools asks for assessments of "institutional effectiveness" (Rogers, 1990) and eschews more prescriptive terminology—most associations imply that institutions will be judged in part by what happens to students. As Manning notes, the current "doctrine of accreditation says that institutions . . . are to be assessed against their stated (and acceptable) purposes. Among those purposes . . . must be goals for the educational achievement of their students. Thus, assessing whether an institution or program is achieving its purposes includes whether its students are achieving satisfactory educational goals" (1987, p. 34).

How will community colleges respond to the increased attention to student outcomes? Community college educators have welcomed that attention in principle, as an affirmation of their institutions' teaching emphasis (McClenney, 1989). But how outcomes should be documented remains uncertain. Commentators have mentioned several potential problems, including limited resources for assessment and limited research expertise among community college staff members (McClenney, 1989; Gentemann and Rogers, 1987); the vagueness of accreditation guidelines, which as yet fail to provide "a systematic conception of the proper role of assessment in the accreditation process" (Ewell, 1992, p. 1); and the tendency of colleges to formulate goals as statements of process, indicating what staff will do, rather than as statements of outcomes, indicating the results to which staff actions will lead (Palmer, in press). A further problem can be traced to faculty, who, with some exceptions in vocational fields, have not developed a professional ethos grounded on documented student learning gains. Few faculty use behavioral objectives to guide instruction and document its effects, nor are faculty evaluated on the basis of student mastery of course material (Cohen and Brawer, 1989).

Challenges to College Leaders

All these problems pose formidable obstacles for college leaders, who must respond by defining the purpose of accreditation at their colleges, securing necessary assessment resources, and fostering the requisite sense of professionalism among faculty. But perhaps the most challenging problem lies in the disjuncture between the occasional, varied attendance patterns of community college students (Adelman, 1992) and the goals orientation of accreditation guidelines that require colleges to specify educational outcomes that reflect overall institutional purpose and toward which all students are to be directed. The associate degree is earned by less than 10 percent of all community college students (Cohen and Brawer, 1989, p. 58). Without the anchor of a common educational end such as a degree, it is difficult to forge a strong link between community college student outcomes and institutional purpose. Community college leaders responding to accreditation mandates either must make a case for an institution whose mandates are open-ended and relevant to the varied goals students set for themselves, or must define institutionally prescribed outcomes toward which student learning will be directed, and reform matriculation processes accordingly.

Both approaches are represented, if not explicitly noted, in the outcomes assessment plans offered to date in the literature, and suggest how community colleges may handle the accreditation task. Some plans imply an open-ended institution, making scant mention of educational goals per se and focusing instead on the development of information systems that regularly monitor the instructional program and its use by students, whatever form that use might take. Other plans imply a traditional, prescriptive, scholastic institution. They seek evidence of student success in meeting specified objectives and tie outcomes assessment to curriculum reforms and matriculation processes that reinforce student progression through an ordered course of studies. The latter, traditional approach is more difficult, requiring community colleges to put aside or modify open-ended accrediting self-studies in favor of criterion-referenced formats that bespeak a purposeful vision of each college's responsibilities toward its students.

Open-Ended Outcomes Assessment

While community colleges are just beginning to respond to the outcomes criteria in accreditation guidelines, a review of two-year institutions' reports about their past outcomes assessment or institutional effectiveness efforts reveals a tendency toward data collection as an end in itself. Many of the reports offer assessment plans that detail procedures for recurrent analyses of programs and students, but few if any reports link the procedures to judgments about the degree to which student achievement goals are met. These open-ended assessments reflect what Hogan (1992, pp. 39–40) calls the "meaningful processes" approach to accreditation, an approach undertaken more as a means of involving the entire college community in ongoing data collection and program review activities than as a summative evaluation of the degree to which student achievement goals are met (the "final answers" approach).

The assessment literature yields three forms of open-ended assessment. The most prevalent draws from managerial traditions and involves recurrent program review and data collection cycles. For example, Kentucky community colleges (University of Kentucky, 1989) gauge institutional effectiveness through a five-year strategic planning cycle that incorporates program reviews, examinations of selected data from student records (such as the grade point average and baccalaureate attainment rates of community college students who transfer to the university), and a series of surveys routinely sent to entering and exiting students, former students (graduates and nongraduates), and employers. Another managerial approach is described by Kern (1990) in his account of the Collin County Community College District's (CCCCD) preparation for regional accreditation. Faculty,

administrators, and staff assessed the institution's status by working together on a Council for Institutional Effectiveness, which marshaled data to
link the college's diverse activities to stated goals and objectives, and on a
Strategic Planning Task Force, which helped college departments develop
one- and five-year plans. Kern notes that the collaborative self-evaluation
process is as important as the data it yields, and he concludes that "the
broad-based involvement of the entire faculty and staff in the development
of programs and priorities . . . of the college adds to the collegial relationship
and atmosphere at CCCCD and also to efforts to achieve improved institutional effectiveness" (p. 26).

A second form of open-ended assessment is an indicator system. Such
systems are sometimes built on the results of college planning and evaluation procedures. The indicators might include rates of course completion,
graduation, transfer, and job obtainment, and other indices of what happens
to students over time. Collated in reports that relate indicators to institutional activities and organize data that are routinely collected by various
college offices but have heretofore remained unaggregated and unanalyzed,
indicators become systems of inward environmental scanning. Indicator
systems usually array data in a matrix with sources of information listed on
one axis and the desired outcomes on the other. For example, Altieri (1990)
suggests a structural model for student outcomes that uses five outcome
categories of internal and external data commonly related to the community
college mission: knowledge and skills, program achievement, learner and/
or sponsor satisfaction, career success or achievement, and community
impact. The model "is designed to match a typical college's data collection
capabilities" (p. 19). Similar matrices are offered by Blasi and Davis (1986),
the League for Innovation in the Community College (Doucette and Hughes,
1990), and the National Alliance of Community and Technical Colleges
(Grossman and Duncan, 1989). Of these, the league's model is the most
comprehensive, posing questions and listing data sources that can help
assessors calculate outcome indicators for each of five community college
missions: transfer education, career preparation, continuing education,
basic skills education, and access (that is, keeping the door of higher
education open). In the area of career preparation, for example, Doucette
and Hughes ask, among sixteen other questions, "Are students achieving a
broad general education?" They suggest that indicators tied to this question
can be drawn from "standardized assessment instruments; [student achievement in] capstone courses; communication and computational skills in
course assignments; observation of ability to work cooperatively; [and]
follow-up surveys of employers" (1990, p. 17).

The third open-ended assessment technique rests on growth in student
learning and development over time, usually measured through pretest-
posttest assessments in a value-added or talent-development format. A

predominant approach has been to assess the skills development of students who complete a minimum number of credits at the community college. The assessment instrument has been the American College Testing (ACT) program's Collegiate Assessment of Academic Proficiency (CAAP), which is designed to measure reading, writing, mathematical, and critical-thinking skills gained during the first two years of college. For example, Oliver (1990) details the plans of a South Carolina two-year institution to build a value-added assessment program using the CAAP, which is to be administered as a pretest in all entry-level mathematics and English classes and again as a posttest to students who complete sixty quarter hours of credit. Armstrong (1991) describes a similar program at a New Mexico two-year college, using ACT's Assessment of Skills for Successful Entry and Transfer (ASSET) examination as a pretest and ACT's CAAP as a posttest. An unknown variable in both cases was the degree to which students would cooperate at the posttest stage.

Data collected through strategic planning cycles, indicator systems, and pretest-posttest assessments are potentially valuable in post hoc examinations of the institution. For example, indicators of student progress over time can fill a badly needed void, augmenting data on enrollments, expenditures per student, and other measures of the magnitude of the educational enterprise. In addition, the involvement of faculty in ongoing data collection can spur faculty inquiry into instructional purposes and effects. Smith (1989, p. 33) cites a Northeast Missouri State University example that uses CAAP to assess learning gains from the freshman to the sophomore year. Noting that student math scores on the CAAP actually decreased over time, the faculty "created several hypotheses about the score declines, tested them," and implemented several reforms in the mathematics curriculum. Value-added scores for subsequent student cohorts increased thereafter.

The usefulness of such assessments depends, however, on the accuracy of the collected data. While the enthusiasm with which colleges describe their planning processes bespeaks, at a minimum, the processes' usefulness in building a sense of community on campus, skeptics question the ultimate results. For example, McClenney notes that, although "survey work and manipulation of existing institutional data" are logical starting points for assessment, they will be of little help if program reviews are "incestuous paper processes which operate principally to preserve the status quo," or if staff do not address the problems of "poorly designed instruments, poor sampling techniques, poor return rates on surveys, difficulty of obtaining cooperation from four-year institutions, and so on" (1989, p. 51). In the case of value-added testing, Harris warns that standardized instruments, though easy to obtain and administer, may say little about instructional effectiveness if they do not test what is actually taught and do not yield results that can be "channeled back to the person teaching the course" (1989, p. 18).

Criterion-Referenced Assessments

Open-ended assessments allow colleges to describe without judgment. They illuminate the educational enterprise without appraising institutional success. Undertaken without reference to goals for student achievement, they apply a rubber yardstick to the self-study process, implying success in any use of the institution and any degree of learning so long as some value has been added. By insisting on relative rather than absolute ends, two-year college educators "have tended to avoid confronting the issue of exactly what is meant by the term 'student success' in the community college context" (Aquino, 1991, p. 9). Criterion-referenced assessments avoid the problems of open-ended assessment by specifying standards of student academic progress and implementing procedures for determining whether those standards have been met. Howard Community College (1991) is a case in point, calculating indicators for each of thirteen institutional goals. All indicators are reported in relation to criteria. For example, one indicator for transfer outcomes is the proportion of former Howard Community College students at Maryland state universities who are in good academic standing. The college reports the indicator for each university in relation to the criterion that at least 85 percent of the former students will be in good standing. Instances in which this target is not met are noted for further analysis.

Some two-year institutions have also called for the criterion-referenced approach in their plans to assess student learning or to link assessment with curriculum development. In these plans, faculty and administrators participate not only as data gatherers and interpreters but also as course and curriculum builders who define the intended outcomes of instruction in ways that link classroom objectives with overall program and institutional goals. For example, the "assessment model" at Macomb Community College in Michigan, described by Blanzy and Sucher (1992), emphasizes faculty specification of course and program outcomes as a requisite to monitoring and documenting student progress. Similarly, Volunteer State Community College in Tennessee has engaged faculty in the specification of course learning objectives and in the use of those objectives to show how individual classes contribute to the general education and major competencies of program graduates (Ward and Marabeti, 1987). In both these situations, faculty license to teach and assess as they please, without reference to overall program and institutional goals, is curbed. As Blanzy and Sucher say, instructors do not own their courses: "There is a right and a responsibility to develop the learning outcomes in common" (1992, p. 6).

The most detailed example in the literature of curriculum-based assessment comes from St. Petersburg Junior College in Florida and incorporates both faculty specification of learning outcomes and institutional procedures to regulate and monitor student flow. The college's institutional effectiveness model, implemented in the 1980s, began with a curriculum restructuring project that required faculty within similar disciplines to establish common learning objectives for each course and to use those objectives to define logical course sequences within each program (Law, 1988; Folger and Harris, 1989). This reexamination of the curriculum was augmented by policies that mandated student skills assessment at entry, required students to complete remediation if necessary, specified a minimum time after entry within which introductory mathematics and English composition courses were to be completed, and stipulated that all courses in the general education sequence include a significant amount of writing. In addition, faculty were given assistance in assessing outcomes at the classroom level and in developing summative evaluations at the program level. The St. Petersburg example, stressing as it does ordered student progress through the curriculum, suggests that the requisite reexamination of faculty responsibilities must go hand in hand with the requisite matriculation reforms that lead students toward a more directed educational experience.

A third requisite is criterion-based testing constructed by faculty according to the learning outcomes they themselves specify. This testing is implied if not actually described in the available documents outlining curriculum-based assessment plans. Most of these plans suggest testing as a summative evaluation for program completers that allows the college to offer evidence of the extent to which degree recipients master expected competencies. An alternative is posed by Cohen and Brawer (1987, p. 120) in their account of the pilot test of the General Academic Assessment (GAA), a criterion-referenced test of student knowledge in the arts and sciences that was developed with the input of faculty and staff from four urban community college districts. Unlike summative evaluations, which assess individuals' learning, GAA results apply only to student cohorts. The test's 336 items are distributed on five forms, each with no more than 69 items, and the forms are administered to samples of students. When the GAA was administered to a sample of 8,026 students at the urban institutions cooperating in the test's development, results verified a positive curriculum impact, showing a high correlation between liberal arts knowledge and the number of liberal arts courses completed. Cohen and Brawer offer the GAA as an example of how faculty can relate student achievement to curriculum goals, but they concede that the long-held tradition of testing as a means of sorting individuals will block acceptance of tests that assess student cohorts.

Balancing the Responsive and the Prescriptive Institution

It is difficult to draw firm conclusions from the outcomes assessment plans available so far. Current plans are largely tentative outlines of intent, providing information on college approaches to outcomes assessment rather than assessment results, and the success of these plans cannot yet be ascertained. All that can be said with certainty is that the rhetoric of assessment, as represented in the large body of literature calling for institutionally based studies of student outcomes, far outstrips the as yet nascent attempts to put assessment plans into action.

Disjuncture. The two outcomes assessment approaches described in the literature—one based on information collection as an end in itself, the other based on predetermined indices of student learning and attainment— suggest that community college responses to the new accreditation criteria arise from two competing visions of institutional purpose. The first posits the institution as a responsive community service agency in which there are as many outcomes as there are students. The second posits the institution as a scholastic enterprise that prescribes curricula leading to mastery of the knowledge expected of degree holders and to eligibility to advance to the next level of education or to enter the labor market.

The first vision is the less challenging. It ignores the question of educational goals beyond the provision of courses and programs. Hence, there is no disjuncture to bridge between community college students' varied attendance patterns and accreditation guidelines that specify educational outcomes that reflect overall institutional purpose. Conversely, the scholastic approach is marked by a sure sense of the result of the community college experience. Determining what that experience will be requires college leaders to confront the disjuncture head on, seeking avenues of common learning within the context of the open-access institution.

Resolving Disjuncture. There are approaches community college leaders can take to resolve the problem of evaluating students with different goals in terms of an institutional goal. One such approach is to engage faculty in defining common educational ends that will be pursued in all courses and thereby experienced by all students, regardless of the depth of their exposure to the institution. General skills instruction is often the commonality that is sought. Goals established for Lansing Community College, for example, stipulate that reading, writing, speaking, and listening skills will be emphasized throughout the curriculum. To assess goal attainment, all surveys of current and former students include questions about the extent to which teachers have challenged students in these areas (Herder and others, 1990). General education may also weave seemingly disparate courses together. Cohen and Brawer's hypothetical general education model (1989) is an ambitious example of this interweaving. The model envisions a core set of faculty charged with the responsibility of creating general education modules for all courses offered by the college. Assessments would then correlate general education knowledge (however defined by the faculty) with the number of courses students have completed.

A second, admittedly more controversial, approach to resolving the apparent disjuncture between student and institutional goals is to offer continuing education and the more traditional degree programs within different college units, thereby separating out occasional students from those pursuing a curriculum. Criterion-referenced assessments keyed to expectations for student achievement could be applied to the latter students, with faculty working increasingly as curriculum builders along the lines discussed earlier. Cohen and Brawer (1989) have long advocated this separation, arguing that student expectations and needs in the two areas are essentially different. While Cohen and Brawer's suggestions may once have seemed far-fetched, they may take hold as legislators allocating funds to higher education systems take an increasingly dim view of subsidizing the occasional learning of community college students pursuing personal interests.

Neither of these two approaches is easy. They demonstrate the substantial academic and organizational challenges to the open-ended institution that are posed by demands for information on student outcomes. These challenges may or may not result in major changes in community colleges, where acceptance of occasional students has been long established and defended, but they at least should cause educators to question where open-endedness should give way to scholastic prescription. Bringing this question forward will be a salutary byproduct of otherwise difficult assessment ventures.

References

Adelman, C. The Way We Are—The American Community College as Thermometer. Washington, D.C.: Office of Educational Research and Improvement, U.S. Department of Education, 1992. 79 pp. (ED 338 269)

Altieri, G. "A Structural Model for Student Outcomes: Assessment Programs in Community Colleges." Community College Review, 1990, 17 (4), 15–21.

Aquino, F. J. "Operationalizing a Student Typology: Steps Toward Building a Community College Success Model." Paper presented at the annual forum of the Association for Institutional Research, San Francisco, May 1991. 21 pp. (ED 336 023)

Armstrong, J. "Assessing Skills from Placement to Completion." Paper presented at the North Texas Community College Conference, Nov. 1991. 46 pp. (ED 342 437)

Bemis, J. F. "Regional Accreditation." In K. E. Young, C. M. Chambers, H. R. Kells, and Associates, Understanding Accreditation: Contemporary Perspectives on Issues and Practices in Evaluating Educational Quality. San Francisco: Jossey-Bass, 1983.

Blanzy, J. J., and Sucher, J. E. "Technology: The Silent Partner in the Advancement of Measurement and Assessment Practices. A Student-Centered Assessment Model." Paper presented at the Winter Institute on Community College Effectiveness and Student Success, Jacksonville, Fla., Jan. 1992. 10 pp. (ED 342 446)

Blasi, J. F., and Davis, B. S. "Outcomes Evaluation: A Model for the Future." Community College Review, 1986, 14 (2), 53–57.

Cohen, A. M., and Brawer, F. B. The Collegiate Function of Community Colleges: Fostering Higher Learning Through Curriculum and Student Transfer. San Francisco: Jossey-Bass, 1987.

Cohen, A. M., and Brawer, F. B. The American Community College. (2nd ed.) San Francisco: Jossey-Bass, 1989.

Doucette, D., and Hughes, B. (eds.). Assessing Institutional Effectiveness in Community Colleges.

Laguna Hills, Calif.: League for Innovation in the Community College, 1990. 63 pp. (ED 324 072)

Ewell, P. T. "Outcomes Assessment, Institutional Effectiveness, and Accreditation: A Conceptual Exploration." In *Accreditation, Assessment, and Institutional Effectiveness: Resource Papers for the COPA Task Force on Institutional Effectiveness*. Washington, D.C.: Council on Postsecondary Accreditation, 1992. 75 pp. (ED 343 513)

Folger, J., and Harris, J. *Assessment in Accreditation*. Atlanta, Ga.: Southern Association of Colleges and Schools, 1989.

Gentemann, K. M., and Rogers, B. H. "The Evaluation of Institutional Effectiveness: The Responses of Colleges and Universities to Regional Accreditation." Paper presented at the annual conference of the Southern Association for Institutional Research and the Society for College and University Planning, New Orleans, Oct. 1987. 23 pp. (ED 290 392)

Grossman, G. M., and Duncan, M. E. *Indicators of Institutional Effectiveness: A Guide for Assessing Two-Year Colleges*. Columbus: Center on Education and Training for Employment, Ohio State University, 1989. 25 pp. (ED 325 193)

Harris, J. W., Jr. "Assessing Institutional Effectiveness." In S. C. Cowart (ed.), *Project Cooperation: Designing and Implementing Models of Outcomes Assessments for Two-Year Institutions*. Washington, D.C.: American Association of Community and Junior Colleges; Iowa City, Iowa: American College Testing Program; Washington, D.C.: National Council on Student Development, 1989. 76 pp. (ED 321 825)

Herder, D. M., Gwynn, V. N., Burke, I. H., Edmunds, P. A., and Milton, K. M. "Instructional Quality Assurance at Lansing Community College." Panel discussion presented at (1) the International Conference on Teaching Excellence, Austin, Tex., May 1990, and (2) the Consortium for Institutional Effectiveness and Student Success, Toronto, June 1990. 90 pp. (ED 320 634)

Hogan, T. P. "Methods for Outcomes Assessment Related to Institutional Accreditation." In *Accreditation, Assessment, and Institutional Effectiveness: Resource Papers for the COPA Task Force on Institutional Effectiveness*. Washington, D.C.: Council on Postsecondary Accreditation, 1992. 75 pp. (ED 343 513)

Howard Community College. *Assessing Student Learning Outcomes: Performance Accountability Report*. Columbia, Md.: Howard Community College, 1991. 85 pp. (ED 337 227)

Kern, R. P. "A Model Addressing Institutional Effectiveness: Preparing for Regional Accreditation." *Community College Review*, 1990, *18* (2), 23–28.

Law, W. D., Jr. *Quality Control and Institutional Effectiveness: An American Perspective*. Coombe Lodge Report, *20* (7). Bristol, England: The Further Education Staff College, 1988.

McClenney, K. "Student Assessment Practices in the Community College: Current State, Desired State, Getting There from Here." In S. C. Cowart (ed.), *Project Cooperation: Designing and Implementing Models of Outcomes Assessments for Two-Year Institutions*. Washington, D.C.: American Association of Community and Junior Colleges; Iowa City, Iowa: American College Testing Program; Washington, D.C.: National Council on Student Development, 1989. 76 pp. (ED 321 825)

Manning, T. E. "The Why, What, and Who of Assessment: The Accrediting Association Perspective." In *Assessing the Outcomes of Higher Education. Proceedings of the 1986 ETS Invitational Conference*. Princeton, N.J.: Educational Testing Service, 1987.

Mather, J. "Accreditation and Assessment: A Staff Perspective." *North Central Association Quarterly*, 1991, *66* (2), 397–405.

Oliver, S. L. *Making the Vision a Reality. Project Cooperation Demonstration Site Model: Assessment of Student Learning and Development from Entry Through Exit and Transfer to Four-Year Colleges*. Columbia, S.C.: Midlands Technical College, 1990. 23 pp. (ED 322 980)

Palmer, J. C. "Planning Educational Goals and Indicators Around Student Outcomes." In A. M. Cohen and F. B. Brawer (eds.), *Managing Community Colleges: A Handbook for Effective Practice*. San Francisco: Jossey-Bass, in press.

Rogers, J. T. "Assessment in the Southern Commission on Colleges." *North Central Association Quarterly,* 1990, 65 (2), 397–400.

Smith, T. B. "Outcomes Assessment in Action: The Northeast Missouri State University Experience." In S. C. Cowart (ed.), *Project Cooperation: Designing and Implementing Models of Outcomes Assessments for Two-Year Institutions.* Washington, D.C.: American Association of Community and Junior Colleges; Iowa City, Iowa: American College Testing Program; Washington, D.C.: National Council on Student Development, 1989. 76 pp. (ED 321 825)

University of Kentucky. *Institutional Effectiveness. An Overview of the University of Kentucky Community College System, Part Seven.* Lexington: University of Kentucky Community College System, 1989. 95 pp. (ED 340 452)

Ward, J. K., and Marabeti, H. B. *Defining Course Outcomes and Assessment Procedures: A Model for Individual Courses.* Gallatin, Tenn.: Volunteer State Community College, 1987. 43 pp. (ED 296 768)

Young, K. E. "The Changing Scope of Accreditation." In K. E. Young, C. M. Chambers, H. R. Kells, and Associates, *Understanding Accreditation: Contemporary Perspectives on Issues and Practices in Evaluating Educational Quality.* San Francisco: Jossey-Bass, 1983.

JAMES C. PALMER is assistant professor of educational administration and foundations in the College of Education, Illinois State University, Normal, Illinois.

Effective presidents set the stage for accreditation long before the accreditors arrive; leading by example, they build consensus, empower faculty and staff, share governance, and accept criticism collegially.

The President's Role in Building Internal Consensus for Accreditation

Evan S. Dobelle

In college presidents' candid and private moments, when they reach beyond the public phrases about the tremendous value of self-study as a component of strategic planning, it is fair to say that many presidents remain less than enthusiastic about the prospect of an accreditation cycle. After all, on its face, the accreditation process may appear as a challenge to both the president's temperament and his or her short-term goals for the institution. Accreditation review demands campuswide introspection and self-criticism. For college presidents, held accountable in competitive and fiscally challenging environments, introspection may appear to be an unaffordable luxury and institutional self-criticism an undeserved personal affront. Moreover, like many chief executive officers, college presidents often feel pressed to focus on short-term budgetary and programmatic concerns rather than on the longer-term structural issues that are the cornerstones of successful institutional self-studies.

An impending accreditation review can also generate a less than enthusiastic response from faculty and staff, rightly troubled by the thought of additional burdensome committee responsibilities and reports without discernible impact or utility. Thus, far too often, the accreditation process is reduced to an exercise that has low sight lines and generates little in the way of self-examination or a sense of institutional purpose. In extreme cases, preparing for another round of self-study can lead to a campuswide venting of concerns that magnifies existing tensions and reduces institutional cohesiveness while raising serious questions about the college's accreditation status. At the other extreme from the nay-sayers are the converted who view the self-study process as an institutional panacea that in and of itself can lift a weak or foundering campus or inspire a strong campus to new heights. But yea-sayers with such unrealistically high expectations can prove as unwittingly damaging to long-term institutional health as nay-sayers. At the very least, inability to recognize either the true potential or true limitations of the accreditation review process can diminish a college, leaving scars that may last for years as painful lessons of failed leadership.

Practical Leadership Considerations

My goal in this chapter is not to analyze the specific requirements of the accreditation process. These can be found in the well-organized, extensive directions and guidelines provided by the accrediting associations and in related literature. Nor do I seek to justify the philosophical, political, and educational merits of accreditation. As a college president, I accept its importance. Moreover, I believe accreditation does offer institutions regular moments for thoughtful reflection. Instead, I offer a set of six practical, mutually reinforcing considerations to others who are ultimately responsible for leading colleges through the accreditation process. These considerations are (1) building and maintaining consensus before the eleventh hour, (2) building consensus based on empowerment, (3) reaching beyond empowerment for accountability, (4) creating an appropriate organizational infrastructure, (5) formalizing management of the planning and accreditation process, and (6) working toward shared governance. This chapter focuses particularly on the role of presidents in building and sustaining institutional consensus before the actual accreditation process. The six considerations are not a magic formula for successfully engaging accreditation, but they do provide a sensible framework within which to develop internal endorsement for the project. In building this endorsement, presidents set the stage for collegewide renewal. They also prepare an institution not only for meeting accreditation's formal requirements but also for growing in its sense of self and clarity of purpose.

Setting the Stage: Before the Accreditors Arrive

Just as successful political campaigns begin long before a formal announcement of candidacy, a college's accreditation efforts should begin well before the formal notification of a review. Any administration that leads an unprepared and unfocused institution into an accreditation review has already failed the test. Sudden lurches toward institutional self-examination do not constitute leadership; periodic yet unsustained commitment to accountability does not equate to vision; and a mad dash toward collegewide consensus in the face of an evaluation visit does not define self-study or planning.

Build and Maintain Consensus Before the Eleventh Hour. Self-study should complement collegewide planning, with each planning cycle growing out of and integrating lessons gained from a preceding self-study effort.

The challenge facing campus leadership is to define a planning process that maintains consensus around institutional identity, provides regular measurement of progress toward agreed-on goals, allows for adjustments in the face of unforeseen events, and leads directly toward the next self-study. This challenge demands more time than most presidents have to give and offers less immediate gratification than completion of a new building or establishment of a new program. The truly outstanding leader, however, recognizes that development of such a seamless planning and study process promises to leave a responsive, healthy institution as a legacy to the next generation.

Nearly every college president has appropriated the language of strategic planning—far fewer have successfully implemented it on their campuses. And even fewer have developed planning models that both meet the needs of campuses and fit seamlessly with the self-study process. In developing a meaningful planning and study process, the best presidents rely less on the latest textbook fad and more on their understanding of their colleges' unique assets and needs, as well as on their feel for the strengths and weaknesses of their faculty and staff. More to the point, successful presidents do not wait for a formal self-study before they build a positive working relationship with key faculty. The president who attempts to build campuswide consensus at the eleventh hour before accreditation or seeks spontaneous generation of support for a planning process on the eve of self-study may survive. However, he or she will earn no credit on the leadership scale and do little to enrich the institution.

Day in and day out, too many presidents treat their faculties in a manner that calls to mind the story told of a meeting between the late Governor Earl Long of Louisiana and a freshman member of that state's legislature. Rising to the full measure of his capacity for intimidation, Long told the young legislator that, beyond everything else, it was the latter's responsibility to support his governor.

"Governor," said the young representative, "when you are right I will support you. But when you are wrong I must stand on my principles."

"Son," Long responded, "when I'm right, I don't need your support."

Strong presidents recognize that their first test of leadership is not to seek support for their personal positions but to unite a disparate campus around common values and move it toward achievable goals that represent those values.

Build Consensus Based on Empowerment. For presidents who successfully pass the first test of leadership, consensus is in place long before the accrediting team arrives on campus. However, passing this test is much easier said than done, else why do college presidents last about as long as baseball managers? To develop sustainable agreement on campus, presidents must constantly balance human and symbolic initiatives with organizational moves that create a shared sense of mission and a feeling of real empowerment. In unifying a campus around common mission and goals, the best presidents recognize that the actual planning process is less important than the level of empowerment it inspires in faculty and staff. The paradox of successful presidencies is that presidents who sustain power over long periods of time do so by sharing that power throughout the college community. Even the most elegant planning process will not maintain consensus over the long term unless the president uses that process as a means of enabling the college community to shape its own destiny.

Reach Beyond Empowerment for Accountability. Beyond empowering faculty and staff, presidents should push for a planning model that builds in accountability. Academic institutions have been slow to accept performance indicators and effectiveness measures. While presidents and senior staff alone must not define or create the accountability measures, presidents must press for faculty and staff development of these measures as part of their institution's evolving planning process. Such a campuswide effort is never easy. But it is far better to go through the discomforting yet ultimately beneficial process of establishing a method of self-measurement than to wait until notification of an impending accreditation review, when additional anxiety will be added to the discomfort.

Create Organizational Infrastructure. Successful presidents understand the need to build an organizational infrastructure that simultaneously supports planning and self-study and ensures continued faculty empowerment and regular accountability measures. Although every institution demands a somewhat different infrastructure, certain key positions set the groundwork for strategic planning. These positions are institutional research staff, the chief fiscal officer, and the chief academic officer. I have deliberately stated these positions in the reverse order of their traditional importance in the administrative hierarchy in order to emphasize the importance of functions that are frequently overlooked yet essential to the planning process.

A strong, appropriately equipped institutional research office is critical to long-term planning. In difficult budgetary periods, institutional research is often ignored or insufficiently endowed; yet without a skilled professional staff that reaches out to the college as a whole, using appropriate hardware and software, it is impossible to secure necessary demographic, academic, and economic data in a form conducive to analysis. And without this analysis, it is impossible to ensure that the college's mission remains current and institutional goals appropriate and attainable.

Fiscal services are the second organizational cornerstone for successful planning. Too many community college presidents consider their chief fiscal officers to be bean counters who are little more than super accountants. But today's chief business officers must do more than balance their colleges' books. Schools need financial administrators who can build the fiscal management systems necessary to track institutional performance and provide sound advice about resource allocations, assuring that funding exists for priorities identified in the planning process.

The chief academic officer is perhaps the most critical administrative position in terms of advancing outcomes measurements and academic accountability. The vice president or dean of academic affairs must simultaneously serve as an ombudsman for faculty concerns, as the administration's chief spokesperson for curriculum innovation, and as the president's day-to-day link to the faculty. No position after the presidency is more important in the maintenance of campus consensus. Unless the president and chief academic officer speak with one voice, share a commitment to openness, possess the ability to listen and grow, and act willingly on appropriate criticism from within the institution, consensus will soon become an empty promise.

Formalize Management of the Planning and Accreditation Process. Presidents should make management of the planning and accreditation process a formal responsibility. Who is accountable for managing the planning process is less important than that the person bring high visibility and credibility to the job along with the ability and drive to make the process succeed. I have seen institutions where this responsibility has fallen to a vice president of planning, a vice president of academic affairs, or a senior faculty member on released time. While I prefer the first option, a variety of models can work. What is more important is that planning be organized, that it be ongoing, and that it be made a priority by the college and its leadership.

Work at Shared Governance. Finally, in building sustainable consensus on campus, college presidents should focus hard on shared governance. Many presidents talk a good game, but not nearly as many practice what they preach. In fairness to these presidents, far fewer faculty take responsibility or seek accountability when these roles are available even though faculty often persist in arguing that they lack a meaningful role in institutional governance. Overcoming faculty inertia when it exists is, of course, part of the challenge for presidents committed to faculty participation in college governance.

Strong shared governance maintains a common vision over the long term because it allows administration and faculty to rise above individual egos and grievances and attend to the business of institutional standards and vitality. This result depends to some extent on institutional form and structure but even more on the good faith, character, and personal vision of those who shape the institution's future. An impending accreditation review should cause little discomfort to the president who has taken the often uncomfortable and admittedly risky steps necessary to build campuswide consensus around values, mission, and goals; who has established meaningful shared governance and an environment of open communication; and who has set in place an ongoing planning process that ensures accountability.

Concluding Caveats

Presidents leading a college into a useful self-study effort would do well to keep a few basic thoughts in mind. First, self-study is no time to get cute. College presidents must fight the temptation, however great, to find a positive spin for every facet of the college's performance. A less than candid approach to self-study undermines both the integrity and utility of the planning process. Moreover, every campus has a few disaffected faculty or staff members who will invariably point out even the best-concealed weakness or failing, and nothing arouses the ire of an accrediting team more than the suspicion that a college is covering up something. In the long run, dishonesty is even more damaging to the relationship between administration and faculty than to the accrediting process. It is tragic to see a president who has worked hard to establish open communication on campus lose his or her hard-earned credibility in an attempt to skirt the truth at accreditation time. Candor, even when it hurts, is an important message of this chapter.

The second thought is that solid college presidents begin self-studies with a clear understanding of what accreditation is and what it is not. An evaluation report is not a measure of how good or bad an institution might be—an institution is as good or bad as it wants to be. Nor is an evaluation team a hit squad sent in to bring down a college or administration mired in controversy; colleges do not need hit squads to end controversy. Nor is the end result of an accreditation visit ever an instantaneous redefinition of the college's mission and a reenergizing of the campus community; new definitions and energy have to come from within. Instead, accreditation is simply one formal measure of how well a college is meeting its expressed mission. It is not a value-laden exercise, merely a check that the college's mandate is being met according to generally acceptable standards. As such, the self-study process offers a useful moment of reflection on performance. It is not, however, a substitute for ongoing planning.

Third, as is pointed out by other chapter authors, successful presidents put a great deal of effort into selection of the self-study committee chair. In my experience, presidents who claim to be "faculty presidents"—and most do—should encourage appointment of the chair from within the faculty. The chair should understand the difference between self-criticism and self-flagellation. He or she should be credible as a faculty spokesperson and not be thought of as the voice of the president. He or she should also possess the organizational skills necessary to carry out self-study logistics and be amply bolstered with secretarial and other clerical support.

Last, strong presidents understand that their role in accreditation is to stay in touch with the process without attempting to manage it. They set the groundwork and then lead by example: they remain open, accept fair criticism collegially, and ensure that the visiting accreditation team is approached with candor and respect.

EVAN S. DOBELLE is chancellor and president of the City College of San Francisco.

Small colleges' accreditation costs may be proportionately higher than those of larger institutions; however, accreditation benefits can be substantially greater as well.

The Impact of Accreditation on Small Colleges

Eduardo J. Marti

The process of accreditation greatly affects small colleges because, on the one hand, the demands accreditation makes on limited fiscal resources and faculty time have disproportionate repercussions in small institutions (McCoy, 1976; Vineyard, 1978), while, on the other hand, because of their size, smaller schools can reap the advantages of necessarily involving a large percentage of their population in the preparation and analysis of the self-study report. Also, when a small college in a small town is evaluated, it becomes the center of attention and receives some real benefits from that attention. And, finally, accreditation may better validate the quality of a small than a large school because standards of excellence may be more uniformly applied throughout the institution. This chapter explores how the process of preparing for an accreditation visit affects small colleges. It pays particular attention to making the best use of limited resources and to the appropriate college response to the review agency's report, whether positive or less positive.

Preparation for Accreditation

Approximately a year and a half prior to the accrediting team visit, the college president receives a letter outlining a timetable for the visitation process. A set of guidelines for preparation of the self-study report accompanies the letter. Usually, the accrediting agency also holds a training session for individuals who are in charge of or will participate in the self-study.

Selecting the Self-Study Committee and Chairperson. The president's first task is to select a steering team of individuals who will produce a document that describes how the college is fulfilling its mission and stated goals. The committee that is selected must be representative, and, because resources are necessarily limited in smaller institutions, the president must rely heavily on the willingness of faculty and staff to participate. If sufficient resources are available, the team chairperson or document editor may receive released time from teaching or additional compensation for his or her efforts. It is tempting to place the burden of compiling and editing the self-study report on an administrator, particularly someone from the president's immediate staff, such as an executive assistant or academic dean. I strongly suggest that the president resist this understandable temptation. The strength of a self-study report lies in its ability to accurately represent institutional commitment to the college's mission and goals. External evaluators will quickly detect an administrative hand in the writing, and, as honest as the report may be, the fact that it is written by a representative of the administration can sow seeds of doubt about the document's credibility in the minds of the visiting team members.

The president has much to gain by entrusting the preparation of the self-study report to a faculty member who understands the institution's mission. While this person need not be an enthusiastic administration supporter, he or she should not have an axe to grind and should have the respect of his or her colleagues. One of the advantages of a small college environment is that the college president knows most employees and therefore can select the self-study chairperson directly, rather than rely on others' knowledge of the faculty. Another advantage is that the self-study steering committee can be truly representative of the institution. Since these committees usually contain between ten and fifteen individuals, the self-study group can easily represent one-quarter of the entire college faculty and staff.

President's Role. The president's most important task after appointing the self-study committee is to create a timetable for periodic reports and a climate of support for the committee's efforts. After the initial contact with the self-study steering committee, the president should step back and play a less active role, becoming merely another institutional information source for the committee when required.

One of the drawbacks of small size, in this case, is that the president cannot easily avoid contact with the individuals writing the report. Thus, without intending to, the president can easily influence the self-study report and the college can end up with a document with an administrative flavor. It is incumbent on the small college president to make every effort to step aside in order to ensure that the document represents the findings and reflections of the institutional community.

In preparing for the accreditation visit, the college president should influence the process, not the result. He or she should (1) educate the staff about the importance of accreditation, (2) seek volunteer faculty, staff, and administrators to serve on the self-study steering committee, (3) name as chair a teaching faculty member who is not viewed as the "president's person," and (4) stay out of the process and ensure by example that the senior administration does the same.

Cost of the Visit

The accreditation visit is a major expenditure in a small college. Money for this visit should be reserved over time so that there is no need to squeeze the operational budget to pay for site visit expenses. Obviously, this is easier said than done. However, there are rewards as well as costs, and small colleges can reap valuable benefits from the visit, perhaps more so than larger institutions, where relatively few participate in the compilation of the self-study and the external review visit itself. If a college community feels positive about the generation and distribution of the self-study report and if it has had the opportunity to discuss the report in open meetings, chances are that the visit itself will become an occasion for celebration in which all can take pride, and costs need not be exorbitant.

At a small New England community college where I served as president, a steering committee member proposed placing welcome baskets in visiting team members' hotel rooms. What was particularly touching about this suggestion was the committee's organization of a college group to assemble the individual baskets. This was not only a welcoming gesture to the evaluators but also a positive expression from the college community that was communicated to the team. Traditionally, in the Middle States region, the evaluation team is welcomed at a Sunday evening dinner that includes both team members and the campus individuals with whom they will meet. Institutions with sufficient resources usually hold this dinner at a restaurant or other formal setting. Schools with fewer resources can find this obligation onerous. I have reduced the fiscal outlay a number of times by having the dinner catered at a college facility, whether a converted general purpose room or the college cafeteria. I like to think that our not going to extravagant lengths to wine and dine the team became a positive factor in the evaluation process. This way of arranging the dinner is even more ideal when the dinner is planned by members of the college community instead of the president's office. In some cases, steering committee members have supplied desserts and pastries. I have always dreamed of having the entire dinner prepared and catered through the culinary talents of the entire college community. Obviously, however, such participation depends greatly on the institution's climate and culture.

In sum, presidents of small colleges should minimize costs but provide a pleasant atmosphere by (1) planning ahead, (2) adding a local touch to welcome the visitors, (3) providing comfortable but not luxurious accommodations, and (4) remembering that computers in the rooms will be more appreciated than wine at dinner.

Presidential Activity During the Visit

The small college president should understand that the accreditation visit is not an evaluation of his or her personal administrative skill but of the entire college community. Therefore, the president's role during the visit is that of a host respectful enough to stay out of the process. Presidential responsibilities and activities during the few days of the visit are usually restricted to making welcoming remarks during dinner, making statements when asked by the team during the normal course of the visit, and making preparations to receive the final report. At the same time, it is imperative that the president be available during the entire visit, especially to deal with any unforeseen crises or unusual team concerns.

In short, the president serves the accreditation review process during the site visit by being available but not intrusive. He or she is (1) a good host, (2) remote from review activity, except when needed, and (3) ready to respond to a crisis.

Exit Interview

One of the greatest advantages to undergoing an accreditation review in a smaller institution is that the entire college community can be involved in the exit interview. An open setting for the exit interview helps members of the self-study committee share the fruits of their labors with their colleagues and involves faculty and staff more closely in the results of the external evaluation team's recommendations. Most external team chairpersons are willing to deliver the oral report of strengths and weaknesses before a comprehensive audience. I believe that this makes the evaluation team accountable to the whole college and makes the whole college a partner in the evaluation process.

However, the president should caution the college community that they will be present at the discretion and courtesy of the external team. Therefore, they should not expect to ask questions during the oral report. By the same token, the president should alert the external team chairperson that representatives from the larger community may be present, so that the chairperson can prepare an exit report to be heard in an open setting. The team's oral report is confidential. If particulars of the team's exit interview are requested by the internal or external community, the president is entitled to withhold comments or releases on the premise that the review team's findings are confidential until delivered to and accepted by the accreditation commission. Moreover, the president is responsible for alerting the college community to the fact that, although team members may present their findings about strengths and weaknesses, they will not present their recommendation for accreditation or reaccreditation at the exit conference.

After the Exit Conference

The president's greatest challenge in the accreditation process may come after the exit conference. Sometimes the president receives a written copy of the visitors' report at this point, without the confidential recommendation about accreditation. This is the time for the college to respond to any factual errors in the report. It is also the time to surmise the accrediting team's final accreditation recommendation, basing the surmise on the areas identified for institutional improvement. However, nothing should be released to the press as yet, since the accreditation commission has yet to conclude its actions.

Public Disclosure and Public Relations. After the exit interview, it is highly appropriate to discuss the accreditation process and results of the final conference with the board of trustees at a regularly scheduled board meeting. Since board meetings are open, this meeting provides an opportunity to reaffirm that the exit interview was confidential and that the evaluation team's findings are as yet tentative. On receipt of the letter indicating the accrediting commission's ultimate action, it is imperative that the president and his or her staff be ready to report the accreditation outcome to the press, the business community, and appropriate advisory bodies. This is an extremely important moment. Accreditation enhances public trust in an institution. Accreditation of a small school supports school statements about institutional quality and equalizes some of the differences between the school and larger institutions, particularly when both are reviewed by the same accrediting commission. Since all colleges accredited by the same commission are measured by the same standard of excellence, it behooves the small college president to point out that his or her institution has been tested by equal qualitative measures. Peer accreditation usually provides a small college with the opportunity to increase its visibility in the larger community by claiming an accreditation status identical to that received by larger colleges and universities.

Public relations strategies should include news releases and, where possible, press conferences. The accreditation of the local college is big news in small and rural areas, so it should be easy for the president and staff to orchestrate a public relations campaign that focuses on the accreditation visit and results. This is a good time for the president to publicize the arduous process the college undertook in preparing for the review and to underscore for the public the ramifications of accreditation for the institution and the community it serves. Notice of accreditation also creates a wonderful opportunity for the president to reaffirm the institution's quality to its state or local funding sources. Finally, accreditation results should be shared with local and state legislative and government representatives so that they in turn can reassure their constituencies that they are judicious keepers of the public coffers that fund higher education.

Recruitment. Accreditation can help a small college in recruiting students, and the statement of accreditation is an important part of any college or university catalogue. However, some small colleges also create a special recruitment brochure or flyer, calling attention to the significance of their accreditation in terms of credit transferability and a quality education that is recognized by the college's peers, who have found that the college meets or exceeds the standards of excellence set by the accrediting board.

If the Report Is Less Than Positive. When a report has negative elements, it is important that the president be candid. He or she should not withhold information from the press. The more an institution tries to do so, the larger the headlines and the impact of the story as told by ever more curious reporters. In addition, a president can usually bank on the probability that there is someone inside or outside the college who will take advantage of a less-than-positive review to further his or her own agenda. Therefore, it is best to get in front of the story by being proactive and reporting frankly to the college community and then to the community at large about the accreditors' recommendations.

The recommendations will specify areas for improvement, and these problem areas must be clearly articulated to the college community and plans quickly designed to correct them. Rapid and decisive presidential action in this regard reminds the trustees and the college community that the accrediting commission's judgments result from and reflect on the entire college and not only the president's office. Difficult though it may be, a college president should not act as though he or she takes the accrediting commission's decisions personally. Obviously, however, in the face of a less-than-positive judgment from one's peers, a president should take immediate corrective action. To best exercise damage control, he or she must demonstrate strong, positive leadership in the development of responses that effectively address the accreditors' concerns.

Whatever the accreditation outcome, the college president must take charge in ways that will confirm his or her effectiveness. He or she should not hide but should (1) provide accurate information to the press, (2) be extremely clear about plans to correct cited weaknesses, (3) assign only one person, either the president or a designee, to speak for the college, (4) ensure that the board of trustees and the college community are aware of the accreditation situation prior to releasing information to the press, and (5) remember to thank those who did the hard work of preparing the self-study report, including support staff and steering committee members.

References

McCoy, W. H. *Position Papers: Task Force of the Small/Rural Community College.* Washington, D.C.: American Association of Community and Junior Colleges, 1976. 19 pp. (ED 165 843)
Vineyard, E. E. *The Invisible Wall: A Report on the Status of the Rural Community College in America.* Washington, D.C.: American Association of Community and Junior Colleges, 1978. 28 pp. (ED 161 581)

EDUARDO J. MARTI is president of Tompkins Cortland Community College in Dryden, New York.

Well-designed outcomes assessment can change the academic decision-making culture from opinion based to information based.

After Accreditation:
How to Institutionalize
Outcomes-Based Assessment

G. Jeremiah Ryan

Confronted by internal opposition and external pressure, academic administrators face a challenging task in implementing outcomes assessment systems. One would think that measuring outcomes is plain common sense. However, on many college campuses, faculty and staff expressions of discontent, confusion, and opposition suggest that the concept of outcomes assessment is easily misunderstood and its implementation frequently distrusted.

Internal and External Climates

Outcomes assessment is a concept to which most campus constituencies pay much lip service but little real attention. For a college community to agree on the yardstick by which its graduates and faculty should be judged, college members must take a big step away from their familiar hierarchical definitions that measure success through courses passed and degrees obtained. For even the most competent and highly regarded teaching professor, outcomes assessment is often scary. Consequently, calls for outcomes-based determinants of student achievement rarely come from inside academe. Despite administrative appeals to common sense, faculty often see the push for outcomes assessment as anything but common sense. It is not unusual for faculty to charge that outcomes assessment is yet another administrative attack on tenure and academic freedom or yet another attempt at garnering evidence for reducing faculty ranks. It is also not uncommon to hear old arguments resurrected about selling out to business or caving in to government bureaucracy.

Because they are focused on the internal climate, faculty do not always hear the ever more frequent choruses of external demands for change heard by administrators. The regional accrediting commissions are becoming more and more explicit in their requirements for outcomes-based reaccreditation reports. State postsecondary agencies, whether coordinating or regulatory in nature, are increasingly forcing schools to, as the agencies say, comply with accountability standards—a bureaucratic way of saying that they too want outcomes reports. Most importantly, the businesses that hire college graduates are questioning these graduates' abilities. Many if not most corporations are challenging colleges to do a better job of ensuring that graduates have nontechnical job-related skills, such as being able to read, write, and think. Industry-based technical advisory committees are telling faculty and administrators that college graduates often lack basic preparation—a complaint sometimes followed by the exasperated observation that the business sector would gladly give the new graduates the necessary technical training if only they could read and write.

Compliance Approach

The external climate requires academic administrators to implement an outcomes assessment system; the internal climate requires that this system be one that all campus constituencies will accept, or buy into. Thus the administrators' task is a difficult one, and when state mandates, accreditation requirements, or business demands finally move a college to consider outcomes assessment, administrators must make a strategic decision about how to proceed. A tempting and ready option is to comply only with the letter of the law by administratively producing the necessary reports. This compliance approach spares most of the faculty and staff from even the most remote association with the reporting requirements, and satiates the agencies that are requesting data. The college that selects this option usually assembles a small task force of trusted senior faculty and staff to review the mandate, acknowledge the president's and the chief academic officer's desires to keep the requesting agency off the college's back, and examine whatever compliance data can be assembled. The information is packaged, sometimes creatively enough to be used on campus as a report of institutional success, and the requisite report is mailed off. With luck, it will thereafter gather dust in a filing cabinet or on a shelf.

The compliance approach meets external reporting requirements while producing little if any effect on the internal academic environment. The college selecting this option has chosen the quickest, easiest, and least expensive route. However, it also has missed a wonderful opportunity to change from opinion-based to information-based decision making.

Student Success Approach

An alternative to adopting the compliance approach is to transform the faculty's view of outcomes assessment as a valueless nuisance into a view that a worthwhile measure of the educational enterprise can be achieved through emphasis on student success. In this approach, the academic administrators' role is to sell outcomes assessment as an enhancement of the educational process, not a sellout to business or government. Administrators must carefully demonstrate how outcomes assessment can improve the learning process without compromising academic freedom or jeopardizing faculty job security. The collegial and deliberative habits that characterize the traditional college governance system should be viewed as helpful instead of harmful to this effort to transform faculty and staff views.

The student success approach is more expensive, more time consuming, and more controversial, but ultimately more productive, than the compliance approach. There are seven principles that I have found extremely useful in implementing the student success approach and developing outcomes-based assessment and information systems for campus decision making. Because it is always helpful to understand the inherent perils of any new approach, I have incorporated some discussion of these perils into the seven principles.

Use appropriate terminology. Words are important cultural symbols, perhaps more so to academics than nonacademics. If outcomes assessment is to become a reality, academic leaders must be sensitive to terminology. Faculty have become increasingly jaded about and distrustful of such terms as *outcomes, assessment, accountability,* and *total quality management.* A hallmark of academic excellence is careful and thoughtful use of language. Therefore, buzzwords should be avoided at all costs. Faculty will more likely join the outcomes assessment effort if it contributes to their basic role of teaching students. The more they are involved in the design and implementation of an effort with direct classroom impact, the more enthusiastically they will embrace it. What does this imply for those who seek to evaluate outcomes? First, find an acceptable term for the effort. I have suggested *student success,* since this term focuses on the ultimate customer and on an end held in universally high regard. Whatever term is chosen, it should be campus based and teaching based, not derivative and empty of meaning to those who must build the system it describes.

Pledge amnesty. Before faculty will take outcomes systems seriously, senior leadership will have to pledge amnesty. Specifically, this means that no one will be criticized, demoted, or fired based on the assessment process or results. Senior administrators must insist that the major intent of the outcomes program is to improve institutional effectiveness and not to create a stalking-horse for a reduction in force. Practicing amnesty is difficult. It requires composure under criticism, toleration for ideas of often limited merit, and the ability to continually encourage ideas from people known to be obstreperous, uncooperative, or uncreative. The faculty, rightfully so, will take any of the following actions as signs that amnesty is not being practiced: breaking confidences, ignoring an idea, public or private denigration of an idea or its originator, punishing the originator or the originator's supervisor for the suggestion, treating a serious proposal humorously, or refusing to listen to future suggestions from an originator. By contrast, the following actions will be seen as helpful and conducive to open discussion and toleration of difference: thanking the originator, rewarding the initiative, overlooking imprudent thinking, praising good ideas, and quickly adopting the workable suggestions.

Integrate the system. When a new idea arrives on campus, a college's first instinct is to respond decisively by creating an ad hoc committee, task force, work group, or team, usually with a formal title. This step gives the new arrival the high organizational profile it deserves, conveying its importance through the energy and resources dedicated to it. Too often, however, such organizational responses leave academic departments, governance structures, and other important components of the college's traditional decision-making system out of the loop, or bring them in only at the end. For outcomes assessment to develop on campus and, more importantly, for it to work, the full decision-making structure has to be integrated into the organizational response. The integration should take place at the beginning of the process, not the end. College, academic, and faculty leaders should jointly develop the plan for design and implementation of the outcomes program. The veteran political observer might call this approach co-optation. The entrepreneurial academician might think of it as the development of ownership in the product. However this collaboration is viewed, what evolves from it will probably be a hybrid of new groups and old systems. A new committee will probably spearhead the implementation process and watch its progress, but the members of that committee will probably be the traditional campus doers and thinkers, now dedicated to the outcomes concept.

Understand the different roles of macro and micro analyses. It is an old debate: Which is more important, the department or the college? And the answer is still the same: both. Administrators should take care to demonstrate that the outcomes system, whatever it is called, is the most vital component of such ongoing institutional processes as strategic planning, program review, and annual reports, because it provides information on student success. Collegewide measures of outcomes are important and increasingly required by one or more external agencies. Program faculty, however, play little role in collecting and analyzing data related to these macro measures. The measures of collegewide success that are not defined by the faculty should be presented only as guidelines for academic program evaluation. Teaching faculty must identify the more specific micro measures most important to their programs and define benchmarks of success. Most likely, each program will have different sets of success measures because of intrinsic program differences.

Collect information, not data. After the dedication of faculty and staff time, the most important investment a college can make in outcomes assessment is the production of information, not data. Thanks largely to the reporting requirements of external agencies and the marvels of computer information systems, most colleges today are data-rich beyond imagination. Yet they remain information-poor. Many outcomes systems lack faculty support because faculty identify them with unintelligible data dumps of hundreds, if not thousands, of pages of green computer paper. Workable outcomes systems focus on presenting relevant information in readable, sometimes graphic, formats. If an outcomes system is to be accepted by faculty, there must be near-universal acceptance of the reliability and intelligibility of outcomes information. Faculty acceptance is based less on the college's investment in hardware, software, and research offices than it is on the development of user-friendly reporting formats and the routine availability of personnel to interpret data.

Be persistent. The first question the campus skeptics often ask about outcomes assessment is, Who cares? The second is usually, How long will anyone care? Watching the sometimes frequent changing of the administrative guard, faculty have a tendency to be cynical about the staying power of an outcomes assessment system. The persistent use of outcomes information by academic officers will signal that assessment is not merely a trend but an important component of the institutional science. Academic administrators, therefore, need to demonstrate the system's continued importance by constantly paying attention to the information produced. Read it. Question it. Use it. Challenge it. Publish it. Distribute it. Ask for interpretation. Make outcomes information pivotal in academic decisions. Do all of the above continually. Change the decision-making culture from one that is opinion based to one that is information based.

Spend resources. The development of a successful outcomes system will probably cost more in personnel, computer time, and research than imagined at the outset. Patience coupled with persistence will pay off. Delays need not be viewed as setbacks. Opposition should not be viewed as defeat. Developing a viable and useful outcomes system requires intellectual commitment, physical stamina, unwavering support, and continual attention.

The Politics of Outcomes

Understanding the importance of the seven principles I have outlined will enable the academic administrator to better prepare for the long-term development, implementation, and internalization of an outcomes-based system of decision making. The politics of outcomes, however, will be much more immediately felt on campus. There are at least seven rules that guide outcomes politics. The first three relate to colleges as open political systems and the last four relate to personal political practices.

Inactivity prevails. No amount of encouragement will result in the active involvement of all faculty in any initiative, even outcomes assessment. College leaders should accept this and deal with those faculty who, for whatever reason, decide involvement is important.

Participation is fluid. Many faculty who do participate in outcomes assessment do so only after they see it as essential and beneficial. To be superior in the classroom, it is not necessary for faculty to have a broad view of education that recognizes the value of outcomes assessment. Nonetheless, college leaders should appreciate these faculty members' participation, however infrequent, as valuable.

Conflict is normal. Campus decision making is fraught with conflict and always will be. Competing interest groups continually coalesce and fragment. The development of an outcomes system will also inevitably lead to conflict. Institutional leaders should view this conflict as healthy creative tension.

Anticipate opposition. The academic leader who undertakes to lead the way in outcomes assessment should develop a list of anticipated objections and strategies for dealing with them and those who raise them.

Facilitate opposition. Yes, it is Machiavellian, but it works. Involve predicted opponents in the development of the outcomes assessment process, and they will develop ownership of the process. Here, leaders must practice the art of compromise.

Do your homework. The academic officer leading the way on outcomes assessment must be better informed and better prepared than anyone else at every step of the process. Remember, in the academic world, ignorance and even innocence are seen as weaknesses.

Delegate. The outcomes assessment process will develop with less opposition and controversy if those faculty and staff charged with the responsibility for determining measures are allowed to assume leadership in terms of planning and implementing a system mutually acceptable to faculty and administration. Academic administrators, therefore, should identify like-minded faculty advocates and empower them to carry out the process.

Implementation of Outcomes Assessment at Harford Community College

Harford Community College, where I am an administrator, is a comprehensive suburban Maryland institution that serves 6,000 credit and 16,000 noncredit students annually. In Maryland, it is considered a midsize school. In terms of its outcomes assessment implementation status, it is probably representative of hundreds of other community colleges. External pressures for outcomes-based accountability are mounting from the Middle States Association of Colleges and Schools (the college's regional accreditor), the Maryland Higher Education Commission, and local employers. Internal faculty opposition to accountability is also significant.

Harford is currently in the process of complying with the Maryland Higher Education Commission's accountability standards and responding to the Middle States Association's recent reaccreditation outcomes concerns. However, we have decided to move beyond compliance and develop real student success measures. A Success Measures Committee is being created, to be charged with recommending a set of institutionwide indicators of student progress. Faculty, in turn, will develop programmatic success measures and benchmarks independent of institutionwide numbers. Obviously, the list of institutional effectiveness measures that could be assessed is endless. Harford has chosen to focus on those related to transfer and career students. We want to better assess their goals and expectations when they enter and their outcomes after they graduate or do not return. Going beyond compliance and understanding outcomes assessment politics are important first steps in the process for Harford. In the end, however, we hope to produce information usable not only for the accreditation visit but also for making good decisions for the college's future.

G. Jeremiah Ryan is vice president for marketing, planning, and development at Harford Community College, Bel Air, Maryland.

*Community colleges and accrediting agencies have a symbiotic
relationship, and accreditors help colleges meet external challenges.*

Accreditation and the Community College: Challenges and Opportunities

Howard L. Simmons

The first junior colleges in the United States went unaccredited because they
were founded around the turn of the twentieth century, before any of the
existing regional higher education commissions. Later community and
junior colleges, however, found accreditation difficult for other reasons. It
was not until the 1930s in the Middle States region that a handful of public
two-year colleges (primarily former technical institutes) won regional accreditation. And it was not until the late 1960s and 1970s that most
community colleges were founded and received some form of recognition
from a regional accrediting body. Aside from the problems associated with
their exponential growth in the 1960s and 1970s, community colleges
experienced a unique set of difficulties when seeking accreditation in this
same period. Central among these difficulties were the lack of real peers to
perform evaluation reviews and the prejudices of those at four-year colleges
and universities who believed that community colleges were not really
colleges.

Today, despite the existence of a large and well-trained pool of peer
reviewers for community colleges, and four-year institutions' recognition of
the community college's importance in the higher education constellation,
thorny accreditation-related issues still exist for community colleges. A
number of these issues are addressed in this chapter. Perhaps the most
critical ones concern the intrusion of external forces into matters that
properly belong to the community colleges and their representatives. I
define *external forces* as those entities that community colleges do not
directly influence or control. These entities include state and federal agencies, other colleges and universities, some accrediting bodies, sponsoring

NEW DIRECTIONS FOR COMMUNITY COLLEGES, no. 83, Fall 1993   © Jossey-Bass Publishers bodies, and even some governing boards. Regional accrediting bodies, however, are not external forces, because regionally accredited institutions, including community colleges, are members of the regional associations and play an important role in shaping the associations' policies and procedures.

Benefits and Limitations of Association Membership

Membership in a regional accrediting association carries with it both benefits and limitations. Transfer and articulation, for example, is an inherently complex issue with potential for contentious debate and interminable conflict whose resolution cannot be mandated because the benefits of transfer and articulation require the voluntary collaboration of community and four-year colleges. Some community college educators believe that their students receive unfair treatment in the area of transfer and articulation, and some in higher education and accrediting circles would agree that significant numbers of four-year institutions still have policies and practices that preclude the unfettered transfer of credits from community colleges—even where articulation agreements have been worked out. However, I do not agree with those who believe the transfer and articulation problem would be resolved if regional accrediting bodies set a "specific mandate in the regional review process for a college or university to take into account the goals set by other local or feeder institutions and the ensuing need for a collaborative response" (Prager, 1992, p. 55). I would argue that such an approach would be not only an infringement on institutional autonomy but also a long-term detriment to the community colleges.

Resolution of the transfer-articulation issue is but one of several needed resolutions that will require the collaboration of community colleges with other sectors of higher education. And as other community college researchers have concluded (for example, Cohen and Brawer, 1987), there are many reasons why student transfer is still a problem. I am, therefore, more in agreement with Prager's call for a national study of "transfer-enabling guidelines" at an early date (1992, p. 58). The Middle States Commission on Higher Education has recently appointed the Task Force on Transfer and Articulation, which includes representatives from all sectors and levels of the commission's accredited membership. Because the transfer-articulation problem is not limited to any one region, the task force will seek input from knowledgeable sources around the country.

Impact of the 1992 Reauthorization of Higher Education Amendments

Typically, the attempts of external entities to mandate higher education policies and practices do little to resolve the issues the policies and practices are intended to address, and complicate rather than simplify institutions' ability to carry out their educational mission. For example, in early 1990, the Inspector General of the Department of Education produced a highly critical report that alleged, in broad generalizations, that accrediting bodies could no longer be considered reliable authorities about institutional eligibility for federal financial aid. Much of the report was based on erroneous assumptions. Its findings were predicated on a relatively small number of institutional abuses in which most of the degree-granting institutions recognized by regional accrediting commissions were not involved. Nevertheless, responding to pressure from the executive branch and from some state regulatory agencies to remedy the alleged problem, the federal legislative machinery developed the Reauthorization of Higher Education Amendments of 1992, a body of law that includes the most intrusive provisions on the autonomy of accredited institutions and their accrediting associations in the history of higher education legislation.

However, the problems of most financial aid abuse and student loan defaults do not originate either in educational institutions or their accrediting bodies. In addition, those of us who must address quality maintenance and improvement strongly believe that a constantly improving accreditation protocol ultimately will do far more to improve quality in higher education than any of the provisions of the Reauthorization of Higher Education Amendments. Therefore, the net effect of this legislation has been to establish equally punitive conditions for both the transgressors (who are few and primarily from the for-profit educational sector) and the nontransgressors (the others in the for-profit sector, and the vast majority of the not-for-profit sector). For example, both the provision for unannounced visits to institutions having a significant number of vocational training programs and the regulation calling for the review of predetermined "high" default rates could have a negative effect on two-year colleges. In addition, and most unfortunately, the latest version of the proposed regulations as of the writing of this chapter would still include community colleges in the category of schools that "offer prebaccalaureate vocational education" and still would require most community colleges to obtain accrediting agency preapproval of changes in the type of program offered or the level of credential awarded for prebaccalaureate vocational education programs. To address these and other defects in the legislation through the rule-making process, two-year colleges, their four-year counterparts, and the accrediting community must take all necessary and legal steps to protect their institutional autonomy and avoid greater intrusion by the federal government into institutional affairs through the institutions' default or inaction.

Accreditors joined the campaign to have accreditation status restored to the federal legislation as a key factor for determining college eligibility for federal aid. In addition, the accreditors worked with the colleges, the Washington-based higher education associations, and the Council on

Postsecondary Accreditation to correct a major flaw in the amendments—the omission of "pre-accredited" or "candidate status" as an institutional category for aid eligibility. This category is of obvious importance to community colleges, since relatively few if any institutions from other educational sectors will be seeking their initial accreditation at this point in the development of U.S. higher education. Community colleges enlisted the aid of their constituents and elected representatives in correcting the omission. If their efforts had not been successful, thousands of deserving students might have experienced interruptions in their programs of study. This vexing case illustrates the symbiotic relationship between accrediting bodies and their members, which is characterized by the two parties' ability to act in concert for their general welfare. Such actions are possible because the accreditation membership develops, approves, and applies the standards and procedures by which accreditation protocols are carried out.

As a result of the intense lobbying activity by some state agencies to diminish the role of existing accrediting bodies in the determination of institutional quality and accountability, the reauthorization amendments also include provisions for a greater state regulatory role. As part of the triad of accreditation, federal, and state interests and efforts, state agencies have a legitimate role in helping the federal government determine institutional eligibility, especially by establishing minimum requirements and protecting the public interest. However, because state agencies are more susceptible to political pressures than accreditation associations and try to achieve results by regulating behavior, they are not in the best position to directly assist institutions in the quest for quality improvement and institutional excellence. Conversely, accrediting agencies operate on the well-accepted and reasonable assumption that real institutional improvement occurs only when colleges and universities make a formal, voluntary, and autonomous commitment to assessing their own overall effectiveness.

Community Colleges' Role in the Assessment Movement

The community college sector is a strong leader in the assessment movement. In 1988, I described how "the still youthful community college" sector had naturally embraced assessment at a time when the meanings of "words like 'excellence,' 'quality,' and 'effectiveness'" (Simmons, 1988, p. 1) were still being debated at all levels of higher education. Much of what is being done today by community colleges in assessing institutional effectiveness and student outcomes is consistent with and complementary to accreditation's overall goal of promoting educational quality and excellence. For example, before it was fashionable to develop assessment programs, Nassau Community College obtained a Fund for the Improvement of Postsecondary Education (FIPSE) grant to critically evaluate its academic programs, and the Middle States Commission on Higher Education used this community college model to assist other community colleges with similar interests in assessment program development. At the same time, California community colleges also received a major FIPSE grant to develop assessment guidelines and criteria.

Although some individuals persist in believing that institutional effectiveness as defined by accreditation standards means meeting minimum standards, most regional accreditors have adopted strong assessment criteria precisely for the purpose of moving beyond minimum standards. As affirmed by other authors in this volume (see especially Dobelle, Marti, and Ryan), colleges that view assessment simply as a necessary but minimum compliance requirement stand little chance of real, qualitative improvement. I believe that increased emphasis on educational outcomes is the most important accrediting change in the last decade. And this emphasis illustrates that accrediting agencies, with the overwhelming approval of their constituencies, have concluded that genuine assessment, by definition, requires an institution to meet more than minimum standards.

This is not to say that a given community college, any more than any other college, automatically has the political will to make the curriculum decisions that make it possible to assess student outcomes and use them as the basis for constructive academic change. However, the general trend toward employing the perspective of outcomes will help answer persistent questions about whether the community college sector has incorporated adequate general education requirements in its program.

Accreditation Expectations for Community College General Education

Meeting the general education requirements embedded in the eligibility criteria and standards of regional accrediting commissions is often a challenge for community colleges for several reasons. These include the time limitations inherent in associate degree programs, the fairly rigid requirements of many state licensure and regulatory bodies, the time needed by many students for remedial and developmental studies, and the politics of degree program distribution.

In light of the restricted time in which community colleges must ensure an effective general education, it is incumbent on accrediting bodies to consider institutional mission, program goals and objectives, curricular balance, curriculum types, and student characteristics when reviewing community colleges' general education outcomes. The difficulty of striking an appropriate balance between the general education and specialized course components of a curriculum sometimes causes accreditors to question whether an institution meets both the letter and spirit of regional accreditation criteria and standards for general education. The more important question, however, is whether community college general education programs are still relevant in terms of program integrity and quality improvement. And since accrediting agencies and community colleges alike are giving more prominence to general education assessment, these questions lead to another that asks if the results of these assessments are being used to maintain and enhance institutional effectiveness.

Some accrediting agencies have been concerned that general education requirements in some community colleges continue to be eroded because of decisions to add yet other professional and technical courses to associate degree requirements. There is also concern about the potentially adverse effect on students of colleges' increasing the total number of credits required for the associate degree, sometimes far in excess of the normal sixty to sixty-four credit range. While some colleges maintain that the additional credits improve quality or increase the likelihood of occupational success, they usually present little or no tangible evidence of enhanced student or program outcomes, thus suggesting that the institution's reviews of its degree programs and their general education outcomes have been either inconsistent or nonexistent.

Maintaining Quality and Excellence in Off-Campus Programs

Community colleges often conduct off-campus credit and noncredit programs as an integral part of their mission. Ostensibly, these programs are offered in response to demonstrated need, making courses available to students who face barriers to main campus matriculation, even though off-campus programs in areas poorly served by public transportation also pose questions of access. Accrediting bodies are generally less concerned with ease of access than with the nature and quality of off-site programs. Of primary concern is the community college's ability and commitment to maintain program integrity, supervision, teaching, and learning comparable to that on the main campus. Community colleges, therefore, have a responsibility to inform accrediting bodies of proposed off-campus programs or proposed changes to existing programs, while accrediting bodies have a reciprocal responsibility to ensure that accredited and candidate institutions are fully accountable for any programs conducted under their auspices. In addition to the specific requirements for accrediting agency evaluation of off-campus programs, the reauthorization amendments also require colleges to notify their accrediting bodies in advance of the establishment of such programs. Certainly, both community colleges and accreditors need to ensure that off-campus programs are included in any assessment or evaluation system.

Maintaining Quality Despite Reduced Fiscal Support

Clearly, most states' fairly severe, successive, and sustained fiscal cuts in the community college allocation have the potential to diminish academic quality. The accreditation community cannot simply ignore enforced budget reductions for planning, self-study, assessment, evaluation, and other peer review processes. However, since budget cuts and cost containment are coming at a time when community colleges are also being called on by state funding and regulatory agencies to provide greater evidence of effectiveness and accountability, it is also incumbent on accreditors to formulate approaches that might assist community colleges and other institutions to take whatever steps are necessary to maintain quality, institutional integrity, mission fulfillment, and adherence to accreditation standards.

Maintaining Learning Resources. When faced with difficult budget decisions, educational institutions often reduce library and other learning resources. Community college libraries and learning resource centers may be least well-positioned to absorb such reductions because a disproportionate amount of their budgets may already be consumed in acquiring costly technical books and journals and providing assistance for nontraditional learners. Community college students often need more assistance than four-year college students in learning how to use library and learning resources, thus requiring that a larger portion of available funds be spent on reference services, bibliographic instruction, and other information literacy programs. Money spent on making community college students information literate and independent learners is indeed well spent. While a smaller, well-selected, and better-used library collection might contribute positively to this goal, community colleges must not cut library and learning resources so drastically that teaching and learning are adversely affected. There are alternatives. Some require cooperation and collaboration among institutions within and across sector lines: for example, sharing resources and providing electronic access to collections and data bases.

Maintaining Faculty Balance. Despite the pressures of declining fiscal resources, ensuring balance in the use of full- and part-time faculty in the community college is critical. In some community colleges the absolute number of full-time faculty has decreased to such an extent that an educationally defensible core of faculty no longer exists for some academic programs and disciplines. Factors that determine an appropriate balance should be taken into account in self-study, evaluation, assessment, and accreditation.

Even though some accrediting agencies have fairly precise definitions and requirements for an appropriate mix of faculty, most shy away from blanket prescriptions. Today's stronger focus on assessment in general raises questions about the extent to which rigid quantitative measures are reliable indices of effective teaching and learning. Nonetheless, accreditation commissions should continue to be concerned about those colleges, including community colleges, that view the use of part-time and adjunct faculty solely as a means of balancing the budget and not as a means of enhancing student learning outcomes.

Struggle to Maintain Institutional Autonomy and Academic Freedom

Because community colleges' very creation is often the result of politicians' making political decisions, and because community college allocations continue to depend heavily on the colleges' close alignment with governmental sponsors' and funding agencies' views, the observations of some regional accrediting commissions, such as the Middle States Commission on Higher Education, suggest that there is more political interference in the management, governance, and operations of community colleges than of other educational institutions.

Threats to institutional autonomy and academic freedom take many forms. They include college personnel decisions made independently of existing administrative and governance systems; awards of outside contracts without regard to internal fiscal controls and ethical standards; and attempted impositions of the values of persons or groups outside the college community in attempts to dictate the nature and content of curricula. The threats can also include external attempts to exercise line item vetoes over a college's budget, even when the items' actual contribution to the budget is small; attempts to hold college budgets hostage as retribution for what is considered too great an exercise of institutional independence; and efforts to censure the speech or actions of individual college constituents or groups. In these and similar cases, the community college usually calls on its regional accrediting association to intervene on its behalf. Even though an association may be limited in the ways it can assist colleges without intruding on institutional autonomy and faculty and staff academic freedom, it has a special obligation to protect member institutions from inappropriate intrusion.

Whatever the circumstances or potentially adverse conditions, the community college has demonstrated its ability to respond well to change. It has given strong evidence of its commitment to assess its own effectiveness and its impact on students. It continues to make the necessary adjustments to meet the new challenges and opportunities offered through its symbiotic relationship with the agencies that function as the community college's own instrument of accountability. This complementary relationship assumes even greater importance in a period when community colleges will continue to be especially challenged by many strong external forces.

References

Cohen, A. M., and Brawer, F. B. *The Collegiate Function of Community Colleges: Fostering Higher Learning Through Curriculum and Student Transfer.* San Francisco: Jossey-Bass, 1987.

Prager, C. "Accreditation and Transfer: Mitigating Elitism." In B. W. Dziech and W. R. Vilter (eds.), *Prisoners of Elitism: The Community College's Struggle for Stature.* New Directions for Community Colleges, no. 78. San Francisco: Jossey-Bass, 1992.

Simmons, H. L. "Institutional Effectiveness in the Community College: Assessing Institutional Effectiveness Through the Accreditation Process." Paper delivered at the League for Innovation in the Community College conference, Charlotte, N.C., July 1988. 16 pp. (ED 297 825)

HOWARD L. SIMMONS is executive director of the Commission on Higher Education, Middle States Association of Colleges and Schools, Philadelphia.

An annotated bibliography on accreditation and the two-year college is provided. It includes publications on self-evaluation studies, educational outcomes and outcomes assessment, and the use of the accreditation process as a planning tool, and general articles.

Sources and Information: Accreditation and the Community College

David Deckelbaum

The accreditation process is often viewed as a time-consuming and costly exercise for determining whether an institution of higher education fulfills the standards put forth by an accrediting agency and meets the goals and objectives contained in the institutional mission statement. Recently, however, accrediting agencies have been requiring institutions to employ outcomes assessment as part of the review process, and institutions increasingly find the accrediting review preparations and the external investigating team's report to be valuable tools for both immediate self-improvement and long-term planning.

The following publications reflect the current ERIC literature on accreditation and its effect on the community college. Most ERIC documents (publications with ED numbers) can be viewed on microfiche at approximately nine hundred libraries worldwide. In addition, most may be ordered on microfiche or on paper from the ERIC Document Reproduction Service (EDRS) at (800) 443-ERIC. Journal articles are not available from EDRS, but they can be acquired through regular library channels or purchased from the University Microfilm International Articles Clearinghouse at (800) 521-0600, extension 533.

General Articles

These articles provide an overview of the accreditation process, including criteria and standards by which institutions are evaluated.

Academic Senate for California Community Colleges. *Accreditation: Evaluating the Collective Faculty.* Sacramento: Academic Senate for California Community Colleges, 1990. 8 pp. (ED 318 524)

The academic senate for the California community colleges developed this series of criteria for use by the Accrediting Commission for Community and Junior Colleges of the Western Association of Schools and Colleges as a basis for developing standards for evaluating a college's collective faculty. Criteria for faculty characteristics focus on (1) the hiring process, (2) preparation in the discipline, (3) staff development, (4) evaluation, (5) assignment and load, (6) effectiveness, and (7) staff diversity, encouraging colleges to strive for racial and cultural diversity in faculty and staff. The final section argues that the ideal measure for evaluating the collective faculty is the degree to which the faculty contribute to students' motivation and achievement.

Academic Senate for California Community Colleges. *Standards for Accreditation.* Sacramento: Academic Senate for California Community Colleges, 1990. 23 pp. (ED 315 137)

The standards for accreditation presented in this paper were developed by the Accrediting Commission for Community and Junior Colleges to measure basic characteristics of quality required of all accredited institutions. The standards are divided into eight areas: (1) institutional integrity; (2) educational programs: general requirements, articulation, curriculum planning and evaluation, and credit and noncredit courses; (3) student services and cocurricular learning environments, discussed in terms of general provisions, counseling services, admissions and records, coordination and administration, and service comprehensiveness; (4) faculty and staff selection, qualifications, evaluation, staff development, and other personnel policies; (5) learning resources, including collection development, accessibility, faculty and staff, and general provisions; (6) physical resources, such as facilities, equipment, and facilities planning; (7) financial resources; (8) governance and administration, including the governing board, administrative services, faculty, support staff, and students.

Anker, M., Conn, E., Germond, J. R., and Weiss, E. *Strengthening the Accreditation Process.* Sacramento: Academic Senate for California Community Colleges, 1992. 24 pp. (ED 344 634)

In 1992, the academic senate for the California community colleges adopted this report on the state's accreditation, and directed the senate's executive committee to work with the accreditation committee to implement that committee's recommendations to the greatest extent possible. Suggestions concerning the composition and effectiveness of visiting teams are included, along with recommendations offered to the Accrediting Commission for Community and Junior Colleges and to the academic senate itself for strengthening accreditation activities. Specific recommendations concern the self-study, the visiting team report, the commission, and the standards. Two related reports are attached. The first, adopted in spring 1990 by the Educational Policies Committee of the academic senate, focuses on accreditation in terms of evaluating the collective faculty. The second lists academic senate resolutions on accreditation from 1979 to 1991.

Berg, E. H., Decker, C. M., MacDougall, P. R., Slark, J., and Villa, A. S. *Handbook of Accreditation and Policy Manual.* Aptos, Calif.: Western Association of Schools and Colleges, Accrediting Commission for Community and Junior Colleges, 1990. 139 pp. (ED 324 056)

   This four-part handbook, developed by the Accrediting Commission for Community and Junior Colleges of the Western Association of Schools and Colleges (WASC), is intended for use by two-year institutions under review, members of evaluation teams, and others concerned with good practice in two-year institutions. Part I reviews the purposes of accreditation, standards, policies, and procedures. Part II describes eight standards for accreditation: institutional integrity, educational programs, student services, faculty and staff, library and learning resources, physical resources, financial resources, and governance and administration. Part III describes three types of accreditation policies: testimonial policies developed by the commission, which define good institutional practices; national policies, which advise postsecondary institutions and accrediting agencies about good practice; and operational policies, which affect the organization and conduct of commission business. Part IV is an appendix that includes a description of accrediting agencies and related organizations, the WASC constitution and appeals procedures, and a glossary of definitions and acronyms.

Waggener, A. T., Southerland, A. R., and Leonard, R. L. "Significant Similarities Between Accredited and Non-Accredited Colleges." Paper presented at the annual meeting of the Mid-South Educational Research Association, New Orleans, November 1990. 13 pp. (ED 326 139)

   This study investigated the relationship of accreditation and institutional characteristics, social-psychological factors of college presidents, and institutional compliance abilities for membership in the Southern Association of Colleges and Schools. It also sought to determine if there were selected differences between two- and four-year institutions. The Survey of Interpersonal Values, mailed to 249 college presidents of two- and four-year accredited and nonaccredited institutions, measured support, conformity, recognition, independence, benevolence, and leadership. Prominent factors related to accreditation were institutional compliance abilities and institutional characteristics. There was no significant relationship between accreditation and social-psychological factors among college presidents. Two- and four-year institutions differed on institutional age, full-time equivalent enrollment, and full-time faculty.

Self-Evaluation Studies

Self-studies are an integral part of the accreditation process that simultaneously provide institutions a genuine opportunity for thorough self-examination and a basis for future planning.

The Accreditation Self Study Report of Los Angeles Valley College. Presented to the Accrediting Commission for Community and Junior Colleges in support of application for reaffirmation of accreditation. Van Nuys, Calif.: Los Angeles Valley College, 1989. 133 pp. (ED 318 497)

This accreditation self-study report was prepared by Los Angeles Valley College in support of its application for reaffirmation of accreditation. Introductory sections review methods of organizing for the self-study, the college and its demographic makeup, and responses to previous accrediting team recommendations. The report is divided into ten sections corresponding to the accreditation standards for goals and objectives, educational programs, staff development and diversity, student services, community education and services, on-campus learning resources, physical resources, financial resources and college funding, governance and administration, and district relationships. Plans of action that respond to problems cited in the self-study are identified in each section.

Cosgrove, J. "Link Self-Study with Strategic Planning." *AGB-Reports,* 1989, *31* (4), 24–26.

Long after St. Louis Community College received the maximum ten-year accreditation from the North Central Association, as this report describes, the members of the college have continued to use their self-study report for planning and self-improvement and to document quality assurance.

Kern, R. P. "A Model Addressing Institutional Effectiveness: Preparing for Regional Accreditation." *Community College Review,* 1990, *18* (2), 23–28.

Kern presents a model for assessing institutional effectiveness within the context of an accreditation self-study, drawing from the recent experiences of the Collin County Community College District (CCCCD). He reviews the Southern Association of Colleges and Schools' criteria for institutional effectiveness and the institutional research, organizational, and strategic planning components of CCCCD's model.

Outcomes and Assessments

Accreditation associations have begun to employ education outcomes and assessments as criteria for consideration during the accreditation process.

Langley, H. M., and Wood, C. C. "An Institutional Model for Assessment." Paper presented at the assessment conference Strategies and Prospects for the Decade, Montclair, N.J., March 1990. 90 pp. (ED 318 511)

This paper describes the actions of Brevard College, a private two-year liberal arts college, after it was evaluated for reaccreditation in March 1986 under the new criteria of the Southern Association of Colleges and Schools. Accreditors' recommendations focused on long-range planning, identification of expected educational outcomes, and development of outcomes assessment strategies. In response, the college conducted a campuswide workshop on educational outcomes, formulated a planning process, and tentatively reformulated college goals. An Institutional Effectiveness Committee, consisting of faculty and administrators, was formed to recommend annual and long-range planning strategies and processes, and means for evaluating each action's effectiveness. Using Ken Yamada's variables for comprehensive institutional assessment, the committee developed an outcomes assessment model.

Maloney, D. S. "Assessment in the New England Commission on Vocational Technical Career Institutions." North Central Association Quarterly, 1990, 65 (2), 381–384.

Maloney describes the New England Commission on Vocational, Technical, and Career Institutions' adoption of a revised standard on program of studies that requires the measurement of educational outcomes as part of accreditation reviews. He explains the revisions that incorporate these mechanisms for accountability in the "Interpretive Guideline" and "Self-Study Outline."

Palumbo, S. "Assessing Student Academic Achievement: Columbus State Community College." North Central Association Quarterly, 1991, 66 (2), 467–472.

This article portrays Columbus State Community College's assessment process and its reflection of the ten characteristics identified by the North Central Association of Colleges and Schools for student assessment programs. It provides information about program development and suggests implementation strategies for other colleges.

Petersen, J. C. "Assessment in the Western Accrediting Commission for Community and Junior Colleges." North Central Association Quarterly, 1990, 65 (2), 401–402.

This article traces the increasing emphasis on the assessment of two-year college student outcomes in each edition of the Accrediting Commission for Community and Junior Colleges' *Handbook of Accreditation* since 1978. According to the handbook, a college must conduct a systematic evaluation to determine how well, and in what ways, it is accomplishing its purposes. Further, colleges must use the evaluation results as the basis for broad-based, continual planning and improvement.

Prager, C. "Accreditation and Transfer: Mitigating Elitism." In B. W. Dziech and W. R. Vilter (eds.), *Prisoners of Elitism: The Community College's Struggle for Stature*. New Directions for Community Colleges, no. 78. San Francisco: Jossey-Bass, 1992.

Prager explores the causes of the qualitative and quantitative diminution of community college transfers, including structural causes best addressed through accreditation. She considers the scope of accreditation and policies and practices of specialized and regional agencies. Prager argues that accreditation can influence general education, faculty qualifications, access, and articulation, and she advocates a transfer-oriented accreditation agenda.

Simmons, H. L. "Assessment! Action! Accreditation!" *Community, Technical, and Junior College Journal*, 1991, *61* (5), 26–30.

This article discusses the role of assessment in community colleges and reviews assessment from the perspective of accrediting bodies. It examines challenges faced by community colleges, including planning strategically, implementing effective transfer and articulation, achieving affirmative learning environments, and fulfilling college missions and objectives when confronted with financial crisis.

Accreditation as a Planning Tool

Community colleges are finding it worthwhile to perceive the accreditation process as an aid to institutional planning and research. Both the self-study and the accreditation report produce data useful for ongoing planning.

Griffin, T., Hall, M., and McClenney, B. "Accreditation as an Outcome of Research, Planning and Accountability: An Alternative Approach to Self-Study at the Community College of Denver." Paper presented at the Summer Institute of the Community College Consortium for Institutional Effectiveness, Vail, Colo., June 1992. 13 pp. (ED 345 805)

From fall 1985 to fall 1991, the enrollment mix at the Community College of Denver (CCD) has grown to reflect the diverse center city population that the college serves, including increases in the percentages of minorities and women. The changing student body presents new challenges to the college's academic and student support programs and has accentuated the need for accountability, particularly at the academic program level. At CCD, as this paper discusses, the outcome of the new need for accountability has not been a self-study for accreditation, but rather a proposed special emphasis study for accreditation. This study will include an overview document, an accountability report, and planning documents. The novelty of the special emphasis study is its focus on information management to make planning and accountability routine at the program level.

Grunder, P., Judd, B., and Wingo, O. *Developing an Institutional Effectiveness Assessment Program: A Collection of Resources for Florida Community Colleges.* Gainesville: Institute of Higher Education and Interinstitutional Research Council, University of Florida, 1991. 40 pp. (ED 335 098)

Recent accreditation criteria established by the Southern Association of Colleges and Schools (SACS) require all Florida community colleges to develop, implement, and maintain a formalized planning, budgeting, and evaluation process that continually examines and evaluates institutional performance within the confines of the institutional mission. Designed to assist colleges in developing an assessment and effectiveness plan, this report provides a detailed review of the SACS criteria for accreditation and summarizes the literature currently available on institutional effectiveness. An introductory section analyzes SACS accreditation criteria as they relate to institutional mission, planning, evaluation, and research. The report also examines the role of institutional research in measuring institutional effectiveness and cites state and federal reports and data bases relevant to institutional effectiveness efforts.

DAVID DECKELBAUM is user services coordinator at the ERIC Clearinghouse for Community Colleges, University of California, Los Angeles.

INDEX

ORDERING INFORMATION

NEW DIRECTIONS FOR COMMUNITY COLLEGES is a series of paperback books that provides expert assistance to help community colleges meet the challenges of their distinctive and expanding educational mission. Books in the series are published quarterly in Spring, Summer, Fall, and Winter and are available for purchase by subscription and individually.

SUBSCRIPTIONS for 1993 cost $49.00 for individuals (a savings of more than 20 percent over single-copy prices) and $72.00 for institutions, agencies, and libraries. Please do not send institutional checks for personal subscriptions. Standing orders are accepted.

SINGLE COPIES cost $16.95 when payment accompanies order. (California, New Jersey, New York, and Washington, D.C., residents please include appropriate sales tax.) Billed orders will be charged postage and handling.

DISCOUNTS for quantity orders are available. Please write to the address below for information.

ALL ORDERS must include either the name of an individual or an official purchase order number. Please submit your order as follows:
    Subscriptions: specify series and year subscription is to begin
    Single copies: include individual title code (such as CC82)

MAIL ALL ORDERS TO:
    Jossey-Bass Publishers
    350 Sansome Street
    San Francisco, California 94104

FOR SINGLE-COPY SALES OUTSIDE OF THE UNITED STATES CONTACT:
    Maxwell Macmillan International Publishing Group
    866 Third Avenue
    New York, New York 10022

FOR SUBSCRIPTION SALES OUTSIDE OF THE UNITED STATES, contact any international subscription agency or Jossey-Bass directly.

OTHER TITLES AVAILABLE IN THE
NEW DIRECTIONS FOR COMMUNITY COLLEGES SERIES
Arthur M. Cohen, Editor-in-Chief
Florence B. Brawer, Associate Editor